A Year in the
Calder Valley

Nature notes by
Simon Zonenblick

Saraband

*In memory of my mother Patricia (1941–2021),
who first encouraged my love of wildlife and
writing, and whose own handmade guide to
British wildlife, created for a nursery nurse
training course, was the first example of
nature writing made known to me.*

Published by Saraband
3 Clairmont Gardens,
Glasgow, G3 7LW

ISBN: 9781913393755

Printed and bound in Great Britain by Clays Ltd, Elcograf S.p.A.

1 2 3 4 5 6 7 8 9 10

MIX
Paper | Supporting
responsible forestry
FSC® C018072

Contents

Foreword

A Year in the Calder Valley takes the reader on an evocative journey through the seasons, from a springtime stroll along the canal side at Salterhebble to a winter trek across Warley Moor marshland at twilight.

In these carefully observed essays, Simon's deep connection with the natural world is apparent. Each piece of writing is precise and rich in alliteration and imagery. We are treated to wondrous, and often witty, encounters with foxes, fungi, slime moulds, herons and the 'celebrity geese' of Sowerby Bridge.

Simon's remarkable eye for detail and lyric language cannot help but captivate the reader. Whether he is tramping through 'miry miles' of mud, or pausing in the summer heat to admire beetles 'ambling along sun-beaten pavements' of Rochdale Road, Simon's prose is transformative, uplifting and alive to the landscapes and wildlife of the Calder Valley.

This beautifully written book is a reminder that the humblest of walks can provide the richest of rewards.

Victoria Gatehouse,
award-winning poet, zoologist

Preface

This collection, spanning a year of Calder Valley nature writing, mainly comprises articles I wrote for the *Halifax Courier* and other local publications beginning at a point when the UK was slowly emerging from several periods of Covid restrictions. It starts with walks in my local area – around Sowerby Bridge and its canals – before gradually taking in a wider span of the valley, from the outskirts of towns like Halifax and Elland, to its remote hinterlands with their moorland mosaics of peatland bog, acid soils, icy streams and reservoirs.

After much consideration of the possible candidates for describing this area – including Calderdale and the South Pennines – I have settled on the term Calder Valley, in its geographical (rather than governmental) sense, because this book is loosely framed around the environs of the river and its offshoots. This panoply of hills, villages, small towns and countryside, shaped by the river running through its heart, is very much the picture of the area that looms instinctively in my mind.

The rambles recounted veer as far afield as Blackstone Edge and Walsden in the far (or wild) west, to places beyond the boundaries of Calderdale, such as Mirfield and Dewsbury out to the east. The bulk of the writing revolves around my immediate stamping ground of Sowerby Bridge, but it also takes in wanders around Warley and the lush Luddenden valley, the stones and bones of barren moors, popular parks in Halifax, and railway journeys tracing the valley's borders with the post-industrial edgelands of Kirklees.

A Year in the Calder Valley

The Calder Valley is rich in biodiversity. I've tried to present a fair assortment of the wildlife to be found in this diverse wedge of West Yorkshire, with its unique geography, its proximity to neighbouring counties and its relatively extreme seasons. But this book is more akin to a diary, in that it mostly features the sights and sounds of the specific days recorded, rather than offering an exhaustive journey through the flora and fauna of Calderdale and its surrounding areas.

With this in mind, I'm conscious also of the many areas left uncovered – the reservoirs and small villages outside Halifax, even the famous Hardcastle Crags (which gets a few mentions here and there) – but rather than cramming these in for the sake of their inclusion, I have confined these essays strictly to places visited during the course of the year. In doing so, I hope not only to celebrate some of the district's well-known beauty spots and landmarks – Shibden Park, Salterhebble, Stoodley Pike – but also to shine a light on some of the less-explored corners of this so varied valley.

I moved to the Calder Valley in January 2012, early in an especially cold winter in which the nearby hills and woodland tracks were powdered in frost and layered in sheets of lethal ice. Within a few days of arriving, I had seen my first green woodpecker, above a stream that trickled down the hills above the woods at Milner Royd. Like a lithe, red-hatted jester, it seemed to jump between the stones that jutted from the water, before shooting up the hill into obscurity amid a blur of grasses and high hedgerows. It seemed a good omen.

There are no woodpeckers in this collection, though I hope their absence will be made up for by the many finches, tits, and gregarious geese flitting and cruising their ways through

Preface

its pages; the big birds of prey, the shadowy crows, the plucky blackbirds and the prowling owls; the cormorants cloaked in spider-black feathers that survey the riverbanks like beady-eyed Batmen, plumed in the colours of the night.

I have shared my sightings of smaller creatures, too, unveiling a wriggling array of invertebrates, whose scurries and slidings paint nocturnal pavements in glinting scales, or the residue of shiny slime. Rabbits, deer and foxes skirt in and out of this story, but many of these moments are the stuff of sounds rather than sightings – the mournful cries of animals at night, the shuffles through moonlit undergrowth – or else are fleeting images of fast-footed foxes or disappearing deer, avoiding human intrusion and taking cover in the sanctuary of hidden woodland worlds.

My home looks out onto the canal at Sowerby Bridge, where, along with an ever-flowing supply of water-loving birds, there is an abundance of beautiful trees that bookmark several of the entries in this book. My canalside walks are a daily education in plant life, and the earliest piece in this book recounts my discovery of a most unusual flower – but that is only one of the many different examples of the valley's plentiful flora that I have tried to celebrate in these pieces.

I am not a naturalist by training. Though an avid bird-watcher, and while holding qualifications in horticulture, I claim no professional expertise in these areas. As such, my reflections are not intended as any sort of authoritative account; rather, they are the observations of a poet and ama-teur naturalist, or nature watcher, notes made by one person through one particular period of time, of a very particular place that is well-known to me.

The area explored throughout this book is enjoying a cultural renaissance, with high-profile pop concerts at the historic Halifax Piece Hall, and with locally set dramas as well as documentaries about life on the canal, or the prowess of its railway or industrial past, featuring prominently on television. More and more people are discovering the joys of the valley, trekking its hills or taking to the water on canal boats. In many ways, you could say the Calder Valley is defined by water – and some would say by rain!

These canals were a key part of a key part of the Calderdale landscape, along which raw materials were conveyed between Yorkshire and Lancashire. By the mid-nineteenth century, they were busy hubs of trade and traffic, even giving rise to human habitation, as families of Irish 'bargees' formed makeshift communities living and working on the boats. The arrival of the railways and motor travel spelled the demise of canals as commercial transport links – while my neighbour remembers coal barges passing along the canal until as late as the 1960s, these once-bustling watery corridors fell into disuse by the '80s. They became abandoned swamps of weeds and mud, until, in modern times, they were restored for recreation.

Now, the canals of the Calder Valley are a neatly maintained network of locks and wharfs, complete with information boards and waterside pubs, and with many-coloured boats drifting along them. The regeneration of this system has paid dividends for nature, with the towpaths dotted by plump ducks, reedy edges combed by gangly herons, surfaces stroked by the graceful glides of cool goosanders. Beneath the water, shoals of speedy fish dance; above, swarm clouds of midges are flying feasts for the swallows that dip and swerve through summer sun.

And then, of course, there are the rivers – the surging life-blood of the valley, weaving and intersecting like the branches of some rain-veined tree, fast, free-flowing becks, rushing streams, tumbling cloughs and thin rivulets snaking down the stone-strewn hillsides.

In Sowerby Bridge, two rivers meet in a merge of frothing water. The Ryburn, a quiet, shy river shimmying through Ripponden and Barkisland, slips through villages and meanders past country pubs. The Calder itself spills messily beneath the town's eponymous bridge, where its sandy atolls are patrolled by crossbreed ducks, or sunbathed on by the local celebrity geese, a family of road-crossing, traffic-stopping characters to which the reader will shortly be introduced.

For much of its course, from its Lancastrian source, where I have watched it spring from moorland grasses, right the way along to where it rolls through the fringes of South Yorkshire and joins the Aire at Leeds, the Calder is a rough-and-ready river, rushing over stones and bashing its way through the valley. Indeed, its name derives from the Old English for 'river of stones'. It is a kind of mighty monarch, having carved the contours of the valley, shaped its trades, enabled the transportation of innumerable goods to swell the coffers of its surrounding towns and villages. But it can also turn traitor to its people. Sometimes the violent river rips its banks in furious floods, submerging streets, turning allotments into something more akin to paddy fields, uprooting trees and disgorging mud so thick it coagulates between cobblestones like black cement.

But the Calder can be gentle, too. Geese slumber on the sandy banks in summer; streams trickle and tinkle through the Copley Valley Green Corridor nature reserve; and in the pretty stretches outside Mytholmroyd, lazy afternoons might be passed in meditative contemplation of the river, watching birds alight on sun-warmed stones. I've seen more kingfishers by the Calder than any other body of water, blue sparks flashing through the bankside trees, or swooshing along the river's surface, skirting stones and sailing downriver beneath canopies of willow, oak or sycamore.

Formed from glacial erosion on a bedrock of millstone grit and carboniferous rock more than 300 million years ago, the River Calder was central to the nineteenth-century industrial heyday of the Pennines. All around the hills and riversides is the evidence of bygone trades – a museum of mills and factories, many of them converted into modern apartments, some decaying structures in varying degrees of dereliction. From the large complex of Dean Clough at Halifax to the myriad dye works and textile mills, the boom trades in carpets, cloth and cotton, wool and worsted, yarn and shoddy were powered by the water of the valley, flowing through its rivers, or trickling down its hills in plentiful streams.

Now, its industrial prowess a thing of the distant past, the Calder chugs through the valley in a freer form, unhindered by traffic, largely uncoloured by pollution. Where once the water ran thick with multi-coloured dyes, or clogged with tar and chemicals, the abatement of those industries and the keen work of environmental agencies have revitalised the river's natural state, and seen the flourishing of wildlife along its banks.

The river and its valley provide the backdrop of these forty-six reflections, though for all of the rural rambles recounted, there are also forays into urban wildlife, and I have tried to present a view of the valley's inhabitants not only from among its hills and woodlands, but from beside its narrow rows of terraces, disused factory-stacks, warehouse yards and apartments in old mills, and along its roads, which climb up to thin, stream-bordered paths on the outskirts of towns.

*

I was wondering recently, if I had to depict the Calder Valley in one single colour, what would it be? Green might be obvious – though the flourishing foliage and leaf-clad trees of summer soon subside into earthy browns and sleety whites. Perhaps blue, for its rivers and canals, though their waters are just as often tinted in the glassy green of reflected trees, or the smoky orange of autumnal leaves. Perhaps the valley would be most at home in the mantle of autumn's rusty bronze, but this would overlook the force of life that swells in its abundance of lush greenery, when chicks and young rabbits herald a new spring, and to ignore the resurgence and renewal of its canals.

Instead, I found myself instinctively arriving at the beguiling mystery of purple – the colour of the thistles arrayed beside our ponds, of the heather toughing out the rain and frost on winter moors, the foxgloves lining rural pathways in their flocks of pinky petals. Purple is the colour of the rich Calder Valley sunsets, of hillsides swathed in violet mist, and the thorn bushes and roses that thrive in our acidic soils. Buddleia bushes push forth their long, conical flowerheads with jewel-like constellations of purple petals, attracting beautiful summer butterflies whose satin wings shine in the amaranthine tint of evening sun. Kate Boyce's painting *Stormy Sky over Stoodley*, which graces the cover of this book, beautifully depicts these hues of the Calder Valley I've come to love.

Springtime in the Calder Valley

These last few weeks, many must have felt a quiet joy in witnessing, at the close of a difficult winter, the early signs of spring. Even those of us who like winter can't fail to appreciate the lighter nights, the unfurling buds and colour slowly bleeding across the Calder Valley landscape.

Outside my window in Sowerby Bridge, the canal towpath blooms with dandelions, daffodils, anemones, primroses. At the wharf and in front of the church, blossom trees are budding, brightening the air with soft kisses of pink, like confetti at a wedding. By the waterside, geese doze in snowy folds of feathers, or clamber from the Calder to the sandy banksides, soon to host broods of goslings. On the towpath, mallards mass like sunbathing tourists.

I've been walking by the canal a lot, and the route from Sowerby Bridge to Brierley is awash with budding trees – from the leaves gradually greening to the long white columns of birches, to the pussy willows. Oval-shaped catkins of green or yellowy fuzz hang in tufted bunches, in and out of which hop blue tits, lapping up nectar. I recently saw my first nuthatch on that stretch, while down by the wharf at Salterhebble, great tits and goldfinches entertain me with their avian acrobatics, springing to the feeders suspended from the trees.

Further on, I was surprised a few weeks ago to notice a small array of what looked from afar like toadstools but turned out to be butterbur – *Petasites hybridus*, to be precise – a small shrub with spikes of purplish flowers, native to Europe and northern

Asia. Now spreading across the immediate vicinity, these relations of the daisy are a boon for bees. Invertebrates are more in evidence now – close inspection of leaves, walls and walkways has recently revealed ladybirds, shield bugs and, on the pavement at the Albert Promenade, my first millipede of the year. On light, lukewarm evenings, occasional butterflies hover above my garden.

All along the canal, trees are dotted with dunnocks, sparrows, solitary robins, restless wrens flitting branch to branch, goldfinches and long-tailed tits, slate-blue pigeons bending branches with their weight. As you head up towards Warley and Luddenden valley, the terrain may be less verdant, but even as rusty orange autumn leaves still clog the paths and woodland walkways, signs of spring are evident. Beneath the boughs of naked trees, newborn lambs totter nervously, the fretted skeletons of hedgerows begin to twinkle with emerging flowers.

There is still a nip in the air, and if forecasts are to be believed we have not yet felt the last of the cold – here in Sowerby Bridge we have had occasional, intermittent snow. But all the same, when you hear the growing choruses of birdsong, see the flowers bringing new colours to towpaths and trees, the bugs, bees and butterflies starting to flutter into view like returning friends, it is undeniable that a change is in the air. As we head deeper into April, all these things, in their own unique and beautiful ways, are flying the flags of springtime in the Calder Valley.

Pigeon Streets

A few yards from my home, a flock of pigeons lives in an alcove squeezed into a stone wall overlooking the canal. An intergenerational, multi-coloured miscellany of the birds coo, flutter, fly back and forth between disused factories and trees, or just scuffle and shuffle across the semi-darkened ledge of their makeshift dovecote. They point nervous heads through the gap, prodding the open air with their gingery beaks.

There are rock doves, the most frequent pigeons; stock doves; wood pigeons, whose willowy pipings serenade the summer woods; slate-blue pigeons; beige, brown-breasted, speckled-winged pigeons; bulbous pigeons; scraggy pigeons; pigeons with burning ochre eyes; lithe, teal-toned birds with hints of periwinkle inking through their feathers. There are pigeons white as snow, and there are sludgy-coloured birds with crumpled plumes.

I first encountered these pigeons when I moved to my current home in March 2015. I often see them swooping over the canal in the mornings, swerving sycamores and willow trees, gunmetal greys against a backdrop of dripping green, or marching in suits of navy blue along the path down to the river. For years they've been my neighbours, regular fixtures during walks to the station or shops.

I've written about pigeons, filmed them, sometimes watched as they take flight down the valley with unexpected grace. But they have always been just one among many birds catching my attention – until Covid restrictions compelled

11

me to remain around the vicinity of home. My enforced proximity to these fluffed-up birds has brought them into closer focus in my mind. Pigeons are much-maligned birds, accused of invading human spaces and, due to their scavenging habits, even compared to rats. But my experiences of these birds have been entirely harmonious, and I for one am pleased to live in an area so profuse in pigeons.

Lately, I have stumbled upon a family of pigeons that is new to me, in the eaves of a Sowerby Bridge back street. Nestling in the pipework of an abandoned building, these quiet, calm birds seem to be undisturbed by human presence and will sit for long periods winking down from walls and crevices. The discovery of these pigeons has been one of the upsides of recent times, when, having to remain close to home, I've been reminded of how wildlife so often awaits us on our very own doorsteps.

Calder Valley Waterbirds

The Calder Valley hosts many birds that thrive on or around water, and I'd like to cast a general eye over some of those seen frequently in the valley. From the large – gangly herons scissoring the water for fish or swooping over Copley nature reserve, geese gambolling along the green, wet edges of Sowerby Bridge – to the small: dippers bobbing over boulders outside Ripponden, wagtails skipping from stone to stone along the Calder, coots, moorhen, gulls and, as we shall see, various rarer characters.

Anyone passing through Sowerby Bridge has a good chance of seeing the Sowerby Bridge geese. Nesting around the bridges over the Calder and Ryburn, these Embden geese are known for incursions into human territory: outside the leisure centre, the taxi rank, strolling along pavements, blocking traffic. Their cousins, Canada geese, are almost as ubiquitous. I watch them from my window, sailing the canal, pecking towpath grasses.

Less numerous are Muscovy ducks – typically poised at the canalside, gazing into water, at Sowerby and Hebden Bridge. These grumpy-looking birds are outnumbered by gregarious goosanders – green-headed males and white-breasted females – whose brownish head feathers look like mohicans. I watch goosanders mostly between Sowerby Bridge and Luddenden Foot, vanishing underwater for fish, re-emerging and often swimming in pairs.

Preferring densely vegetated freshwater, coots and moorhen are more likely to be seen in habitats like the lake at Shibden, or the pond at Copley nature reserve, than by the canal. All with black feathers, they are visibly differentiated easily by their beaks – red for moorhen, white for coots, though chicks of either species sport the former. You will see them on open water pecking for fish, tottering across the bank or prodding their spindly legs in and out of sandy shallows, seeking invertebrates or fruit. Similarly coloured, but much larger, the Calder Valley's cormorants are often seen at dusk, standing sentry on river logs. Gothic-looking, almost prehistoric, the iconic cormorant is like a deity in the Calder Valley's pantheon.

This list is just a snapshot of the water birds that abound in the valley, whose aquatic habitats range from moorland reservoirs outside Todmorden to the eastern reaches of the canal as it threads through Elland, where stately swans sail by like satin flags. Often, though, I needn't stray far beyond my door for avian variety. At the confluence of two rivers, and with a canal running through it, Sowerby Bridge is blessed with birds throughout the year – including a few surprises. Only recently, on a gloomy, wet Sunday, I was crossing the bridge over the Calder when my focus was arrested by a bluey blur reflected on the water. A kingfisher! Flying too fast to hold in view, but a brilliant reminder, as it sped into the distance, of the dazzling diversity of birds attracted to the watery wonderland of the Calder Valley.

The Sowerby Bridge Geese

I first encountered the Sowerby Bridge geese before moving to the town. I was on a bus heading to the primary school in Ripponden, where I worked as a teaching assistant. As we squeezed through the junction at the Royal Lofts, a troupe of white geese marched across the road, cars stopping to let them pass. My class teacher surprised me by saying that what I'd seen was quite normal. 'You will soon get to know the Sowerby Bridge geese,' she assured me. 'They're local celebrities.'

Indeed, they are. Riverbank regulars, often seen crossing roads, the geese have waddled their way to becoming the avian ambassadors of Sowerby Bridge. In her poem 'The Geese of Sowerby Bridge', Victoria Gatehouse depicts them 'patrolling the High Street, ganging up on the corner by The Long Chimney' (now The Loose Goose, a pub whose frontage bears a cartoon image of its feathered namesake.)

On the road, not everyone is as sanguine about their plodding presence as on the day of my introduction. Victoria Gatehouse describes the birds causing 'tailbacks … a twenty-strong gaggle impervious to hoots.' Recently I watched a driver get out of his car and clap one straggler away, so resolutely had it plonked itself in the road.

No one can say when the geese first began to saunter the streets of Sowerby Bridge. Some remember them from the 1950s, when they kept mainly to the water. A retired teacher from Tuel Lane primary school recalls 'the odd one or two' wandering to a nearby bus stop. Other residents tell me a brood nested in the gardens of Haugh End Hall. Apparently, this group was 'turfed out when the previous owner died', around the late 1980s, and started milling around the old market and behind what are now the swimming baths. By the 1990s, it was becoming common to see geese on the streets, even more so when the baths were built, shrinking their immediate habitat. By the time I moved here in 2012, the geese were stars of their own Facebook page, represented on cushions and mugs, even featured on regional television.

If you pass too close, a goose will hiss, opening its beak to reveal a thick orange tongue, especially if young are close by. But generally, the geese are relaxed about the presence of humans, and it's often possible to observe their natural behaviours – perching on the towpath on one leg like acrobatic clowns, nibbling grass or basking in the sunshine overlooking the canal, or crossing its waters with swan-like grace.

For all their street-strolling comedy, these are quite majestic birds when seen close up: snowy folds of feathers wet with raindrops, heads buried in wings as they drowse by the canal, or watching the river through eyes of dusty blue. In tumultuous times, they are a stable presence, fondly remembered images of the past amid an uncertain present. The Sowerby Bridge geese are both entertaining and calming to see – humorous, an unusual sight, yet reassuringly familiar. It's quite impossible to imagine the town without them.

Painting the Town Pink – Blossom in Sowerby Bridge

The blossom in flower across Sowerby Bridge this spring has painted the town soft pink, brightening the canalside and other places with its beautiful, blushing colour.

Every April I look forward to seeing the towpath bathed in the delicate masses of its white and pink petals, fluttering from branches that bend over the lock in long, decorative arcs, like fans of luminescent lace.

Most of the blossom in this valley is cherry, from the *Prunus* genus, which is widespread across North America, Europe and China and Japan – where cultivars have been grown since ancient times.

Cherry blossom is pollinated by bees – perhaps one reason we see so many of them here from early spring – but it also attracts a variety of birds, for which cherry buds are nutritious. After feasting on blossom, a bird's beak is smeared with excess pollen, which spreads widely, making the birds valuable agents of distribution. One bird I notice more than any other gravitating towards blossom is the blue tit, which makes its way through the overhanging flowers, dancing in and out of the sugary pink shade by the waters of the canal at Sowerby Bridge.

But blossom trees also bloom well beyond the canal. Around the outskirts of Sowerby Bridge, I'm delighted by their splashes of colour on suburban streets, and seeing the trees begin to bloom outside Christ Church, Wharf Street, always feels like a sure sign of spring.

One other sighting of 'blossom in the Bridge' that lifts my spirits is the small tree in a car park on Wharf Street, which I used to look forward to seeing from my window when living opposite. Its pink petals emerge from early April, surrounded by grey concrete and cars, but against a backdrop of dramatic hills, and brightening many a rainy afternoon with its rich, rose-coloured beauty.

Hawthorn Heaven

As spring blends into summer, among the loveliest sights must surely be the hawthorn trees, which bloom in batches of ten to eighteen flowers, whose snowy colours attract a wide variety of invertebrates and birds. Walking by the canal, I've watched these small, hardy trees slowly coming into flower through May, both as single trees and trained in a hedge-like habit. They beckon bees and butterflies, painting the towpath in beautiful sprays of blossom.

Crataegus monogyna, part of the rose family, is widespread in Britain and common in the Calder Valley. Its flowers are first seen as tiny balls of enclosed petals, gradually opening out to reveal hermaphrodite blooms. One of the hawthorn's most distinctive features is the rich red anthers – female organs – suspended on thin filaments of icy white and hanging jazzily around the style, which give the flowers a fancy prettiness.

Common names such as Mayflower, May tree and May blossom describe the time of year when this dense, thorny shrub or tree typically flowers, but its fragrant blooms will continue for a while yet, long before dark red fruits – haws – start to replace them around early August. The plant's eponymous thorns are around half an inch long and can cause serious injury, which is why gardeners are well advised to wear thick gloves when pruning hawthorn.

According to the Woodland Trust, hawthorn 'is commonly found growing in hedgerows, woodland and scrub. It will grow in most soils, but flowers and fruits best in full sun.' Most of the hawthorns I see locally seem to thrive by water – one particularly elegant tree of about twelve metres stands above the canal, flowery branches reflecting in the water like bejewelled fingers, and hosting goldfinches, thrushes, blue tits and blackbirds, which find protection among its thick and thorny foliage.

Hawthorn will grow to around fifteen metres and possesses variably shaped leaves, dark green and deeply lobed. Each flower will produce a single seed, and in the colder months the deciduous trees, depleted of their lustrous leaves, become meshes of black branches, brightened only by the berry-like fruits high in antioxidants that sustain many a winter bird, including blackbirds, chaffinches and starlings, along with small mammals such as dormice. To quote the Woodland Trust again, hawthorn 'simply teems with wildlife, from bugs to birds,' and its profusion of white and rosy flowers forms a quintessential sight of spring and summer.

Aquilegias

Aquilegias seem to be springing up all over the valley, both in gardens and in natural spaces, and their carnival of colours always seems to me to be a sure sign of summer.

Native to woodland areas of Europe and North America, aquilegias – whose bonnet-shaped and often downward-facing flowerheads see them nicknamed 'nodding blossoms' – thrive in sun or dappled shade and prefer well-drained soils. Yet something in our predominantly wet climate must suit these tall perennials, which hail from the buttercup family, because their presence is not only regular, but apparently on the increase.

The name aquilegia derives from the Latin for 'eagle' (*aquila*), since the petals supposedly resemble eagle's claws, but I rather feel that the common name 'columbine' is more accurate – it is Latin for 'dove', after the way in which the inverted flower resembles five doves huddling together.

I first started taking notice of aquilegias three years ago, when I spotted them growing in profusion along the canal towpath at Mirfield, and ever since then the aquilegias I have planted in my own garden have self-seeded in greater numbers every year.

The flowers are pentamerous – with five petal-like sepals – and come in plumes of purple, pink, yellow and soft blue. Sometimes they are white as icing sugar, or even deep red. They are hermaphrodite (male and female organs on the same individual plants) and immensely popular with bumblebees and butterflies.

There are around seventy species, and while most of those seen locally will be *Aquilegia vulgaris*, I have also seen the dark red *Aquilegia atrata*, the completely downward-facing *Aquilegia × maruyamana*, and various double-flowering hybrids popping up around the fringes of Sowerby Bridge. One patch of land outside a garden just off Wharf Street is host to a multi-coloured plenitude of aquilegias of many varieties – a crowd of garden escapees swaying in the breeze like florid pompoms from a gala.

We can be sure of seeing aquilegias dappling canalsides, spilling out of gardens and even dotting semi-derelict yards and scrub in their bright fineries of colour, attracting beneficial invertebrates throughout the rest of the summer months.

Canal Walks in Summer

I've spent much of the last few weeks on canalside wanders, particularly near my home: the Rochdale Canal between Sowerby Bridge and Luddenden Foot; or in the opposite direction, the Calder and Hebble towards Elland, Halifax, or Brighouse. In summer, the canal and towpaths burgeon with biodiversity, a far cry from the heave and hustle of their industrial past.

Perhaps most noticeable at this time of year are ducklings and goslings, the latter being either the young of Canada geese or the white, street-strolling Embden geese resident in Sowerby Bridge. It is life-affirming to see ducklings clambering in and out of the canal, swimming around mother ducks in search of grass, or venturing in ones and twos on their first daring escapades beyond parental cover. The Embden goslings appeared almost overnight, like balls of yellow wool brightening the undergrowth. They sunbathed on the towpath, guarded by parents who raise elastic-like necks to hiss at passers-by veering too close. The Canada goslings are adolescents now – half the size of their black-and-white parents, confidently waddling along the towpath gobbling grass. Today I watched a dozen Canada geese swimming in triangular formations along the canal at Brearley.

The largest birds are usually herons, which tread treetops in the breeding season like avian acrobats. These summer evenings they are often seen prowling the towpaths, or perched on boats, watching for fish below – the canal is rich in minnows, tench, carp, and more. Smaller birds are easy to spot too, though. Down the towpath near Tuel Lane Lock you have a chance of seeing grebes, with their fancy head feathers and performing frequent underwater dives. At Siddal, I've watched wagtails swooping over stones at Hebble Brook. On the sandy path at Sowerby Bridge, sparrows snaffle worms, twisting under watchful eyes of grazing geese. Crows and blackbirds meander through the grass, and finches feed on dandelion seeds. Wrens flit branches. Jays and bluetits dip and dive among sycamores. Pigeons dodder through the daisies. Many birds are found amid the berry bushes between the Calder and canal – bushes jewelled with the wings of butterflies, the striped fuzz of honey bees, the small charcoal black of beetles, and the tiny eggs of insects cropping up on tree trunks.

Despite their human-dominated history and the boats tied up along their edges, the canals of the Calder Valley are highly rewarding for the wildlife spotter or casual walker.

Magpies

In Halifax, yards from Wainhouse Terrace – that derelict nineteenth-century structure complete with graffitied colonnade, beside the road linking King Cross with Sowerby Bridge – I watch a spark of blue cruise through the grass. Like a will-o'-the-wisp sheathed in iridescent glitter, the magpie's wing twinkles in the twilight.

Soon, the bird emerges: tail dragging like a long black blade; breast white as ice-cream; cape-like wings that are black, but which, in flight, reveal an outer half almost entirely white. He – for the tail's length suggests it is a he – juts his head, waddling toward the stony terrace as if disturbed by the noise of cars, stopping for extended periods to glance around, somehow always looking slightly disapproving. He gives an impression that the Italianate style of the terrace is not to his taste, or maybe it is just the graffiti.

Magpies are part of the *Corvidae* family – relatives of crows – and are among the world's cleverest non-mammals, capable of recognising themselves in mirrors. They mate in spring, producing eggs of brown-speckled blue, and their diets are omnivorous. Among their familiar characteristics are their *'chac-chac'* song, or the drawn *'tsche-tsche'* of the birds' alarm call. They visit woodlands, farms and gardens, and are non-migratory, usually spending their whole lives within the vicinity of their birth.

I see magpies from my Sowerby Bridge window overlooking the canal: swooping from trees, twig in beak, or hopping bough to bough, a ball of black and white, skimming the willows and birch. They will gather in 'magpie parliaments' of twenty-plus individuals. Magpies offer contradictions: two-tone colours jazzed by flashes of azure; fearlessly pilfering from nests – though not as relentlessly as their rascal reputation suggests – yet sounding the alarm at the sight of owls or cats; plodders on lawns or woodland clearings, yet so graceful in flight.

The magpie by the terrace quickens, brushing up towards the dilapidated landmark: chessboard white and black, the violet stripes of a fanned tail, dark wings, opening into frilly white, save for tips tapering like ebony fringes. It seems both dark and jovial – with crow-like shape and Stygian plumage – and as it sweeps up towards the turrets, the magpie could be a bat, haunting the edifice of a ruined castle. But its swooshy tattoos of blue and green lend a jester's essence to this jack-the-lad of birds, which now spreads its wings and goes all but pirouetting through the sunset, above the remnants of faded Victorian glory.

Owl Over Rishworth Moor

Heading over Rishworth Moor this close July afternoon, I am conscious of a distant bird tilting on the wind. As I pound the rough-hewn ground, its stocky shape veers closer, then swings at a kilter, stooping down into undergrowth.

The hills are thistly in colour, a dun brown crimsoned by Yorkshire fog. A motorway throbs by somewhere to the south, its drone no longer heard behind the wind, its long black belt unseen beyond the perpetuity of heath and hills. Above, moon-coloured clouds are massing, as if the mugginess is about to crack open in a downpour of midsummer rain.

No rain comes. But a beating wind still blusters through the grass, carrying the owl on the crest of its wave. It is a chestnut brown shade with white wing tips, and it pummels through the wind, giving as good as it gets, swatting the air with its hatchet-like wings. This is a tough and agile hunter, skimming the ground and brushing through bushes with a lethal speed, circling a hectare of hills in a swooping loop of scything dives, ready to ferret out invertebrates, hook up rodents in its razor-like talons, smacking its grip on necks and puncturing skulls with that blade of a beak, curved in sharp black like a smooth, thin thorn. It is a stubborn, unyielding, ruthless flag, lifting with a wing towards me, one moment manically flapping, the next cruising coolly over stretches of dry grass, rising and dipping, and waiting for its moment.

Yet, despite the violence of its kills, there is a mercy in the split-second paralysis, the severing of spinal cords, the bursting of blood vessels and the piercing of organs, the instant deaths. No torturous truck rides to inhuman slaughterhouses await the prey of this aerial assassin, this pennate population manager swiping over hillock and hollow, painting its predatory arc across the doomy dome of a skyline choked with cloud. This humid afternoon, though, seems to offer no rich pickings. The flight path narrows into a looming hover, and the sullen bird hangs low, brooming through the brow of a hill thickened in green bushes.

Elegantly, the owl soars north, and launches off into the duney distance. For a moment it seems that is the last I'll see of it, dwindling into cloudscape in a shrinking V, before a jolt brings it back into focus. The hungry bird goes shooting behind a chunk of bushy heath, head forwards, beak aimed squarely down, pouncing out of view.

Hedge Brown Butterfly

Like a small, silky shadow, the butterfly floats through wefts of nettle and knee-high grasses; skirts the thistles whose prickly plumes protrude along the riverbank like the headdresses of flamboyant tribesmen dancing in the breeze. I'm wading through undergrowth by the Calder, at Copley nature reserve. It's a warm July evening, after a day of burning sun, and the flowers are thronging with bees and butterflies.

The hedge brown butterfly hovers and dips, too swift to fix in view for long, takes its part in a many-coloured butterfly ballet, as whites and blues, dusky ringlets and brocaded painted ladies pirouette in a parade of summery colour. Though the species are often seen together with meadow browns and others, this particular hedge brown, with its wingspan of around forty-seven millimetres, its bronzed orange wings bordered by a bar of grey-brown and spotted black, seems a solitary spirit hovering above the riverbank.

I try to catch the butterfly long enough to snatch a photo, but this flighty creature is too giddy and restless to be snapped. As it veers further along the brambled bank, though, the hedge brown seems to settle, more at home among the field's edge than in the thick of the meadow. Here, where the slopes peter out into scrub, is the natural habitat of the hedge brown.

Although the Latin name *Pyronia tithonius* refers to the butterfly's fire-like orange wings, its common names – such as brown hedge, gatekeeper and gateway – provide greater clues as to its natural habits. Tending to rest with open wings, it gravitates towards hedges and meadow margins, often nec-taring on the flowers growing by gateways. These include wild marjoram, fleabane, thistles, mint, bramble and ragwort. It is into a profusion of this last plant that the hedge brown I'm fol-lowing is bound.

The sun-coloured florets of *Jacobaea vulgaris*, and its dense growth habit giving rise to fountains of flowers, are not really done much justice by the name 'common ragwort'. As bright and feathery as ragged, these daisy-like yellow are beloved by bees and butterflies, so it is no surprise to see the hedge brown settling to land on a flower at the edge of a bunch. Here, on a grassy tract of land sandwiched between two bodies of water, the hedge brown is in its element, and looks as natural a part of the fancy flower as the buttery, breeze-tickled florets.

As it perches, a coral queen upon her lemon-yellow throne, I am able to capture a photograph, the click of the camera lost amid the chirps of nearby birds. And the butterfly, in its understated beauty, amber wings aflame in late sunlight, seems a perfect image of an English summer evening.

Insect Season

On a recent walk along the canal, some friends and I noted that there seemed to have been more insects than ever around these parts this year. Perhaps it's a combination of the gradual development of trees planted in recent years, not to mention the hot weather – which brings about the imperative of mating – but whatever the reasons I have certainly noticed a boon of invertebrates on the leaves and branches flanking the canal, climbing in and out of riverside flowers, and turning up unexpectedly on roadsides, in fields and woods, over the last few months.

Naturally, there is no shortage of the seasonal regulars – if anything the wasps are outnumbering the bees, and seem to be thriving, along with butterflies, beetles, dragonflies and damselflies whipping past like jazzy shafts of jasper. But I was also introduced to a variety of invertebrates I'd never previously encountered.

First, the cinnabar moth caterpillar, a twisting black and orange tube that feasts on ragwort, and develops into a mysterious looking moth of black and red. Seen close up, its coloured ringlets gleam like lacquered shellac, winking in the sunlight. So zealously do they gobble the toxic ragwort that its toxicity is absorbed into the bargain, making them hazardous for predators to consume.

Although I'd seen evidence of their handiwork many times, I hadn't, until recently, laid eyes on the ashy mining bee – *Ardrena cineraria*, like a little black cola-bottle sweet, but for its cellophane-like wings, and the white rim circling its face.

Large rose sawflies – *Arge pagana* – have carrot-coloured bellies, and dark, transparent wings. They split the stems of roses by weighing them down with eggs. I saw my first hanging around conspicuously on my window sill one late spring afternoon. At least the aptly named brown house moth (*Hofmannophila pseudospretella*) seemed more at home within my home. Unlike sawflies, brown house moths are almost always found indoors and are known to sample cereals and fruits, as well as having a penchant for furniture, fabrics, bottle corks and wood – though my fluttering 'flatmate' seemed content with browsing the juncture of the wall and ceiling.

Lately it has also been common to spot old favourites, like the weevils, shield bugs and ladybird larvae clambering over foliage or scooting over roadside paths. These last are like flecks of black rubber, dabbed orange, and I've seen them in gardens in large numbers. Recently I caught sight of one patiently ascending a towpath tree, scaling the bark with irrepressible energy. Later that same day though, I noticed one exploring an electricity box on a Sowerby Bridge side street.

Closerotomus norvegicus is a creature which happens to go by two of my favourite Latin and common names – the potato capsid. Along with the vegetable its common name suggests, this spud-scoffing bug also commonly feeds on nettles, clover, daisies, carrots and chrysanthemums – and even sometimes cannabis leaves. Fly-shaped, but with two long, arced whiskers that lend the look of an eccentric professor, its sandy brown back tapers to a tiny triangle of green. I've seen it threading through the long grass at the Copley reserve, stopping atop golden samphire, antennae sticking out inquisitively, testing the humid air.

Insect Season

Much smaller than these exhibitionist bugs are the tiny velvet mites – around four millimetres long – cropping up in sandstone walls, or thronging on rotting logs like explosions of scarlet stars, massing this way and that across the wood, each one a squiggle of wriggling ruby, fast-pedalling on the hunt for other small invertebrates. Yet smaller still are the innumerable black grain-like beetles that scrabble over stems and walls throughout the woods, watersides and reserves. Almost everywhere I go, I see them in the weeds, defying identification, seeming to multiply until the very ground we walk on has become a superabundance of invertebrate life.

Beetlemania

The streets of suburban Sowerby Bridge are not an environment I would necessarily suspect as a breeding ground for weevils, yet just the other day, when walking up Rochdale Road, I noticed just such a creature – a dusky brownish beetle with a yellowy spotted rear – ambling along the sun-beaten pavements.

The kerb-crawling weevil is far from the only beetle, or indeed the only weevil, that I have seen in the area of late. A walk along the towpath at Sowerby Bridge sees canalside trees and grasses studded in minute alder-leaf beetles, like smooth blackcurrants, or graced by the glinting greens and ink-blacks of pollen beetles. Developing in buds, these pip-sized pollinators bring no harm to the plants that they inhabit, and they are said by the Royal Horticultural Society to be 'part of the biodiversity gardens support'. Small, dark and metallic, the petite pollen-chompers crowd around in roses and thistles, wolf their way through the offerings of crops, and help to boost the eco-system as they accidentally distribute pollen on their travels.

The land on the town's outskirts, like the scrubby waste ground near the railway station, offers surprises such as stag beetles, skulking through the undergrowth and bearing clawed jaws like puny paragons of pugnacity; with their bull-like heads, they are miniature minotaurs. They bore into burrows, dragging animal waste to their nests to fatten up their young, and in doing so playing vital roles in recycling.

Beetlemania

There are also carrion-feeding rove beetles, their long, dark bodies segmented like iron-plated chainmail. And the extended, somehow clumsy-looking devil's coach horse, which stretches its body through compost, grass and hedges, or creeps under stones to ambush its invertebrate prey: it's a nocturnal predator whose quarry is crushed between pincery mouth-parts. Looking like an inflated earwig, the devil's coach horse, when alarmed, is given to cocking its tail in a scorpion-like pose while ejecting a foul-smelling liquid to deter attackers, and it can dispense a painful bite.

As formidable in appearance, with a big abdomen and menacing frontal pincers, the poetically named *Carabus violaceus* is a beetle of stones, logs and leaf litter, its body a merge of black and purple. Nicknamed 'rain beetle' by some, its commoner sobriquet of 'violet ground beetle' is perhaps a more accurate tag, and it is certainly along terra firma that I have seen these bullet-like beetles. To be precise, I've spotted them on the station platforms, moving along the concrete floor close to a flowerbed, perhaps en route to somewhere to gorge on slugs and snails. Such is the fare of this fast-moving carnivore, for which other delicacies include grubs, worms and weevils.

But beetles come in lighter colours, too, and none more so than the sky-blue weevil I noticed on the edge of Norland Moor, a representative of the *Entiminae* family, or 'short-nosed weevils'. Scurrying by the rocky roadside, it was a fingernail-sized blue bug, long-whiskered and with slatey scales, sliding over stones and nibbling at tiny clumps of grass. The family is widespread, with well over a thousand individual species, but I'd never seen anything quite like it and, when I stopped to take some pictures, I was half convinced the busy blue beetle would be some sort of mirage that might prove invisible to the lens. But I succeeded in capturing it: a flash of cobalt blue, preserved in the photograph for perpetuity.

Treks deeper into undergrowth are like magical mystery tours of diverse creatures, such as longhorn beetles, which feed on plant tissue and whose antennae are often longer than the rest of their bodies. I first noticed them browsing the banks of the Calder at the Copley nature reserve, a typical habitat as they thrive on woodland edges and love thistles. Their bodies caught the evening sun, but it was the curving antennae which were most striking – like long, elastic whiskers banded black and powdery blue. They were *Agapanthia villosoviridescens* – the golden-bloomed grey longhorn – whose distribution spreads as far east as Kazakhstan.

I've seen a definite increase in the reddish-orange soldier beetles, with their oblong thoraxes and long whiskers, whose bodies couple around the florets of thistles in bouts of lust. These soft-bodied omnivores, whose diets take in aphids, pollen and nectar, spend so much of their lives mating that they are colloquially known as the hogweed bonking beetle!

Turning the handle and entering my home on a damp evening in early spring, I noticed a skirting board stippled in small spots every three or four inches. Then I noticed more. Many more. Something about the porch must have attracted them, as it does most years, and before long this little vestibule had become a veritable lair of ladybirds. They spill out onto the balcony, wheel their ways across stems and leaves, hungry for herbivores. These greenfly-guzzling creatures will go so far as to lay their eggs in the middle of aphid colonies, in order to ensure a ready food supply for their newborns.

So ubiquitous are ladybirds, so familiar their waxy, shell-like wing covers, that I admit it rarely occurs to me to take much notice of them, much less scrutinise one close up. So when I decided to inspect one at close quarters, it was like doing so for the first time. The bug I examined was shiny, and wine-like in colour. Moving along the petals of a potted plant, it was a cool, calm assassin, on the look-out for an aphid meal, its back black-spotted, like a domino dipped in blood.

The Latin *Coccinellidae* is derived from *coccineus*, for 'scarlet', and it is, indeed, most common to find red ladybirds with spots of black. But as any gardener will know, the everyday is not exclusive, and it is far from unusual to cast eyes on yellow ladybirds, their backs daubed with dark splotches, or the peachy-pink varieties that are spotted in soft white. But perhaps the most striking ladybird of recent times has been the harlequin ladybird, *Harmonia axyridis*. These larger ladybirds are an arrival from Asia in 2004, and they're becoming ever more widespread. They are also the most variable ladybird in terms of colour, but the ones I've seen ambling through the garden have turned the tables on our image of the species, having pitch black bodies and cherry-red spots.

I've sometimes found that people are surprised that ladybirds are beetles at all, but then the beetles comprise a diverse and numerous order that takes in almost half a million species, and a quarter of all known animal life on Earth. The sandy soils and dryer moorland tops of the Calder Valley seem fertile grounds for them. So often unnoticed as we pursue our busy lives, these familiar, useful creatures are still ubiquitous, skirting the roadsides, haunting undergrowth, inching into gardens and exploring moorland rocks.

A Year in the Calder Valley

With their sleek bodies and distinctive features, from pronged jaws to gangly antennae, and their diverse colouring, the beetles are classic characters of our natural world, and throughout the spring and summer these insects will be busy, rolling over stones along woodland margins, up on the moors, or even beneath blue suburban skies, their burrowing, hunting, pollinating, predating and recycling of detritus helping oil the wheels of biodiversity.

Fungal Forays

Coming across the marshmallowy mounds of thick milk-white and yellow, stuck to the tree trunk like bunched brackets, I felt the kick of seeing something new. Soon, I would learn that the foamy fungi *Laetiporus sulphureus* – common name chicken-of-the-woods – is far from a rarity. Having seen them once, I would notice them more and more throughout this summer, but this first sighting, in the shady tree cover outside Copley, the Calder trinkling nearby, made me wonder if I hadn't chanced on something novel.

Every subsequent sighting of the 'chickens' would reveal them as mostly shelf-like structures, and what I saw at Copley was the initial phase of the fruiting body, before its development into a multiple pile-up. Its knobby body bunched out of the bark and was, in places, indented by tooth-like marks. It was a jumbo fungus, not dissimilar to the bracket fungi – *Ganoderma adspersum* – fastened to sundry trees and ranging in appearance from thin white discs to chunks of soapstone, sulphury and blobbed.

This spring and summer, I've chanced on so many fungi I'd never seen before that the last few months really have felt like a sort of wide-ranging fungal foray. The grass verges by the railway station, in the shade of an old factory and overgrown with weeds, was a breeding ground for toadstools. There I found sundry other red fungi, such as the plump and bulbous *Hygrocybe punicea*, crimson waxcap, and its short, sugary-looking cousin *Hygrocybe coccinea*, known as scarlet waxcap, or the fairytale-invoking scarlet hood, not to mention the profuse scarlet elf cup, whose upturned caps crop up among decaying twigs and leaf litter.

Equally at home among the same dead or shaded undergrowth, the amethyst deceiver – *Laccaria amethystina* – small but striking, beguiled me with its purple colouring. The rubbery hoods of the jelly ears are profuse along the canal near Elland, attached to trees. Tree trunks, whether living or decaying, are ideal hosts for fungi, and I've been amazed at the diversity I have come upon this year, from white balls to prune-like shapes, furrowed and tough, to frilly-gilled brackets, often meringue-white mixed with drizzly grey. My first *Tremella* wasn't very different in colour to these oddities, but most distinct in shape: like gelatinous frogspawn, it was stuck among a bed of wet leaf litter, gelatinous and parasitic, and of 'foliose' shape – boasting seaweedy or leaf-like fronds. It is sometimes known as snow fungus, or silver ear fungus.

At the other end of the colour spectrum, the trees at Willow Hall Dam are host to black King Alfred cakes, also known commonly as cramp balls and coal fungus, a chubby fungus high in toxicity, while on a graveyard wall at King Cross I saw my first ever 'crystal brains' – gum-like splodges of orange and yellow, ranged along a twig.

The roads climbing from Sowerby up towards Boulderclough, Mytholmroyd and surrounding woodlands seem fertile places for fungi – others I've noticed there of late include *Flammulina velutipes* (otherwise known as velvet shank,) and *Clavaria argillacea*, known as smoky spindles, a clump-like fungus sprouting multiple fingery, fruiting bodies, like translucent seaweed, fine and slender.

Closer to home, back in the woods near Copley, I've seen earth balls, warty potato-like characters defined by rough and rubbery flesh, and puffballs, whose barbellate heads lend them the look of sea urchins, and whose fruit body bursts into clouds of powdery spores.

Some fungi I've seen locally have turned out to be in possession of some wonderful names, Latin and common, such as *Schizophyllum commune*, a snowy, coral-like fungi displayed in undulating waves; the diminutive and very accurately titled egghead mottlegill; and the directly designated macro mushroom, whose Latin title is perhaps my favourite mushroom moniker of all – *Agaricus crocodilinus*.

I've given up trying to identify many of the multiplicities of mushrooms assorted round my corner of the valley – the tiny, dust-like parasites staining tree trunks, the tiny pancakes of burnt brown, the milky mushrooms shining like thimbles in a grassy patch near Norland Park. Since this spring, I seem to find them everywhere, in vulnerable-looking ones and twos, or sprawled in groups, and in all settings, from damp woods to twigs and sticks on urban roadsides.

Recently, our valley's Grassland Fungi Project (GFP) told the *Halifax Courier's* Abigail Kellett how fungi 'provide nutrients for plants which support insects, birds and mammals. They also indicate good soil health, which means the fields where they grow are better at slowing the flow of water and reducing flood risk.' They are, though, notoriously difficult to identify, with many deadly species closely resembling edible varieties.

We are fortunate in the Calder Valley to have some rare and threatened fungi on our doorsteps, including waxcaps, whose presences are dwindling in many other areas due to changing practices in woodland management. But our area's notoriously wet weather provides a haven for such rarities. 'We're very lucky,' says Steve Hindle of the GFP, 'to have some incredibly rare species in Calderdale, and some of them have already begun to appear in the fields around Hardcastle Crags.' If my own patch of the area is anything to go by, these appearances show no sign of decreasing.

In Praise of Pond Algae

On the edge of Willow Hall Dam, a small lake on the outskirts of Sowerby Bridge, a raised, muddy area leads into woodland on each side. But straight ahead is another body of water, murkier and shallower than the fish-rich dam, splayed like a patchwork puddle, interspersed with bridge-like fretworks of rushes and twigs. I've tended not to spend much time in this upper area, though it can sometimes be a good place to see a heron stabbing across the mud, or the occasional coot pecking around for aquatic insects or simply crossing the water with an appealing grace. On this clammy summer afternoon, though, I'm drawn to the water's edge by something more unusual, and green.

Like an oily tarpaulin, a thick gauze is clinging to the surface, jelled here, thinning out there, like a goopy custard of carbon-packed gunge, punctuated by stray twigs or rushes sticking out like the flags of amphibious kingdoms.

Crocodile-green, this film of bumps and bubbles is made up of an abundance of algae. The mass forms dense, filamentous mats congealed into a swamp-like substance, green and lumpy as the flesh of a gargantuan toad, clogging the corner of the dam like a giant, wet woolly jumper. In places its green coating is pocked by pores of air, through which the dark cold water below might just be glimpsed, but otherwise it stretches a good twenty or thirty yards wide. It is like a wide viridian sea, a food web hosting insects, snails and other aquatic life, and it is a reservoir absorbing atmospheric carbon.

In sunlight, the algae sparkles slightly, and I notice how the cloak of vegetation is veined in ridge-like grooves. From time to time, a duckling emerges from the reed bed, crossing the quagmire in a cautious, skate-like tread as the mother duck keeps watch among the sedges. The only other obvious signs of life are the blobs of fungi protruding from rotting logs that are half submerged – uneven balls of brown and white, and curious tiny glass-like structures hanging off the sides of decaying wood, stalactites poised above a soup.

Seen close up, one small portion of this chlorophyll mass is like a kaleidoscope of variscite, striated and uneven, an aquatic slab of plasticky zooplankton, peppered with debris of soil and leaves. Taken in the round, it's a viscous substance of melted malachite, a zodiac of different shades of green – a galaxy of algae, which covers a quarter of a pond and rainbows the mire in mosaics of space-age jade.

In the evening sun, as this quaggy emerald city is pin-pricked by softly falling rain, I pick my way over the muddy banks, past streams and lonely bulrushes. The algae's reptilian green is soon lathered in the downpour. Further on, I trace the outline of the main pond. Looming over it are trees whose trunks are blotched in fist-sized globs of King Alfred cake fungus, black as tar. I pick up my pace to head for home, rain beating down in turrets.

Later, when I'm sitting over my laptop in the indoor dry, my mind returns to the green pond algae, its beryl braids of sludge colonising ponds and drenched in chlorophyll, hairs anchored by densely threaded microtubules and fibrous strands. Filtering nitrogen back into the water, this phenomenon of nature offers underwater habitats for many invertebrates, who also feast on the detritus produced when the algae decompose, and, in turn, support the diets of fish, reptiles, birds and more. It is manifestly unjust that such arresting, helpful features of the natural world might be known only by the derisory sobriquet of 'pond scum'. 'Blanket weed' is better, 'green algae' factual but unambitious, 'string algae' scarcely more so, while, of all its nicknames, only the elegant 'silkweed' does it justice. But in the spirit of poetry, I should like to offer my own alternative names for these unusual, unsung, interesting, and frankly quite exquisite wonders of the water. And so, here they are:

~ *froggy yoghurt*
~ *toady tar*
~ *newty nettle*
~ *perennial gook*
~ *pond glue*
~ *turtle soup*
~ *siren's seaweed*
~ *mermaid's wig*
~ *floating-forest-of-filamentous-flagellates*

Gummosis

My first thought was that it was surely some sort of fungi. Splotched like messy jelly against a cherry tree's trunk, orange blobs and yellowy daubs seemed to have appeared out of nowhere, in places spaced apart, elsewhere congealed like squashed fruits glued together. A cautious prod disclosed a texture like that of soft plastic. I wandered home with thoughts of galls and lichen, only for my online appeals for identification to reveal the truth as something wholly new to me – gummosis.

Essentially the secretion of sap from wounds or cankers, gummosis is a fruit tree's response to stress, disease or insect infestation. I have been unable to ascertain any physical damage to the tree in question, though like all its neighbours it is certainly host to a variety of insect visitors, especially small beetles, which seem to enjoy basking in the evening sun against its lumpy lenticels. Specific fungi can also prompt gummosis. The ejected sap leaks through tiny cracks and emerges into hardened blemishes, pimpling the bark like tiny bubblegum balloons.

Struck by the irony of such a pretty addition as gummosis being actually caused by a tree's ill health, I was prompted to investigate the phenomenon. Curiously, the website gardeningknowhow.com described it as a 'non-specific condition' that typically 'occurs when the tree has a perennial or bacterial canker, or is attacked by the peach tree borer'. I have never seen these little larvae, which look in photos like coiled white wires and tunnel deep into the bark to feed, weakening and eventually killing the tree, but I know they are regarded as among the most destructive 'borers' in nature. So strange to think how such infinitesimal interlopers might bring about the destruction of a comparatively ginormous organism as a tree – though every female lays up to about 900 eggs on and around each trunk.

Bacteria is another cause, and I suspect the gumming of the canalside cherry tree was indeed the fruit of *Pseudomonas syringae*, an ingenious bacterium which 'swims' its way through its unsuspecting host with the aid of hair-like appendages. It has been located at the core of hailstones and is even credited as one of the partial progenitors of rain and snow.

The squashy snow sprouting on the cherry tree was hard for me to perceive as anything unwanted or unpleasant. But the more I read of the violence of gummosis, its cancerous advances through tissues, the more I reflected on the cruel ironies of nature, how the attractive may turn destructive. Slowly, the gluey beauty of these citrussy tree trinkets was obscured by thoughts of their sly, viscid villainy, the viscousness of their patient infestations, until what had seemed like small, jolly jellies now leered back at me as poisoned warts – tree-tormenting goblins of gum, a malevolent marmalade bent on deforestation.

And yet it is somehow impossible to truly dislike gummosis – the innocence of its jellybean colours, the novelty of its bold-as-brass splashes on the bark, its downright flashiness. Such is the dichotomy of gummosis – damaging and unhealthy, yet beguiling, the court jester of fruit trees, unrepentant, gaudy and irresistibly kitsch.

Slime Moulds

Just what were these small ball-bearings, studding a tree trunk beside the canal at Sowerby Bridge? Juicy in appearance, squidgy to the touch, they shone in little gangs of orange and ranged in size from the almost invisible to the circumference of a thumbnail. They were slime moulds – wolf's milk slime mould, to be precise, or *Lycogala*, whose fruiting bodies, or *aethalia*, occur as orange, rosy or brown balls, cushiony bumps on damp wood or rotting logs.

A diverse group of organisms that lack a common ancestor, slime moulds comprise almost a thousand unrelated species. Their consumption of microorganisms, bacteria, yeasts and fungi helps to break down dead vegetation. Existing as single-celled loners during times of scarcity, when food is more abundant individuals will coalesce into shapeshifting single bodies, sensitive to chemicals in the air and guided towards food sources.

The late American biologist John Tyler Bonner, a professor of ecology known for his studies of slime moulds, observed how they were 'no more than a bag of amoebae encased in a thin slime sheath, yet they manage to have various behaviors that are equal to those of animals who possess muscles and nerves with ganglia – that is, simple brains.'

Simple and yet complex, the filamentary arrangements of some slime moulds have been compared to the universe's galaxy structure, which in turn has led astronomers to simulate slime mould behaviour to aid their searches for dark matter.

Quite a feat for these small, slimy surprises nestling in the damp, and prized delicacies of beetles and slugs!

The evening after I found this tree, I returned to the scene, half expecting the moulds to have disappeared, so rare and unexpected a sighting as they were. But if anything, they had multiplied. They had colonised a corner of the copse, blistering the birch bark in technicolour bubbles.

Following this first discovery, I've noticed slime moulds elsewhere on the outskirts of the town, on logs in woods and parks, and again among the fruit trees by the edge of the canal, and every time I feel that there is something of the fantasy about them – forbidden fruits, toxic-looking perhaps, though they are harmless.

Slugs and Snails

Like hushed-up folklore figures, they arrived, slippery and silent, khaki-dark. There must have been ten or fifteen smeared across the flagstones of the balcony, and a closer peer at the silent invasion revealed that the slugs were all of a kind: leopard slugs.

Growing up to around twenty centimetres, *Limax maximus* is among the largest of the 'keeled slugs' (a term referring to the ridge that runs along their backs.) However, despite its suffix, it is not actually the largest – that distinction falls to the dark and striped ash-grey slug *Limax cinereoniger*. But on this sultry summer night, it was the leopard slugs that had colonised the walkway, spaced out along the concrete, a marbly myriad of moon-bathing molluscs.

The Calder Valley is a rich environment for slugs and snails – rarely does a summer day go by that my garden wall isn't brooched by the yellowy shells of grove snails, thin and crimpled like boiled sweets, or those of banded snails, sugary cones coiled in cocoa-coloured rings, like ice cream swirled in chocolate sauce.

It was up on Mixenden Moor that I saw my first Budapest slug, a tiny twist tucked between soil and rock, and every day, along pathways and in gardens after rain, I notice different kinds of slugs, from slender strands stretching over stones, to slugs of coppery red, and the large, omnivorous *Arion ater* – sprawled on rainy streets like thick squirts of black toothpaste. Slugs and snails provide such a gallery of diverse colours, shapes and sizes, that I believe the rehabilitation of their reviled reputations is long overdue!

Slugs and snails are active in the warmer months, but often seek shelter from direct sun. The former may retreat beneath vegetation, while the latter may retract into their shells. Snails that I've spotted basking in the grass, or on the drystone walls of farms or graveyards, include the tiny garlic glass snail, with its seven millimetres of brownish shell, the rotund snail – *Discus rotundatus* – whose deep-ridged shells of reddish-brown look like Lilliputian fossils, and the *Cepaea* genus, noticeable for decorative, spiral-striped shells. The most common in gardens, though, are the aptly named garden snails – *Cornu aspersum* – whose bodies of translucent grey-black are loomed over by rusty-looking shells of grazed brown and yellow, and which are eaten by many of our region's songbirds.

When it comes to slugs, night is a good time for sightings, and often I've stepped onto my balcony late on to find the ground mottled in a hopscotch of flubbery rubber: the fluorescent yellow jelly of the *Limacus flavus*, sticky residue scrawled behind it like a gooey glue, and the dusky slug – *Arion subfuscus* – stretched like gloopy tubes of viscid liquorice. Lounging under summer stars are unidentified slugs, some as long as fingers, others minuscule and slim, curling under plant pots or snuck in dark corners, sticky bodies beaded in raindrops.

In the early hours, the paths and pavements of Sowerby Bridge become collages of molluscs, as these silent sliders slither through the starlit streets. They wangle their way under doors, suspend themselves on walls, slide down windows, drag themselves over tiles, or recline among the forbidden fruits of flowerbeds, curled like slimy smiles.

Slugs and snails are part of the natural eco-system, breaking down organic matter and sustaining the diets of amphibians and birds. They also provide us with a dizzying array of pretty colours, caressing the nocturnal pavements in oleaginous delights. From the blubbery beauty of syrupy slugs, to the pearled planets of snail shells, intricately illustrated in crinkled calligraphies of calcium carbonate, the molluscs of the valley never cease to surprise and entertain. While it is fair to say their praises are seldom sung, I believe these slippery creatures are well worth celebrating!

Copley Valley Green Corridor

When plans emerged for a reserve on the edge of a new business park outside Sowerby Bridge, I was initially sceptical. Cited by council chiefs as a consolation for the destruction of trees and the building of houses on floodplain, Copley Valley Green Corridor seemed short-change for the damage caused. And yet, I've come to see the reserve as something of an ecological haven.

Approaching from Sowerby Bridge, you are greeted by a fringe of prickly purple teasel, wibbling in the wind above the riverbank. The reserve is always worth a visit, but it is in summer that it is at its most ecologically profuse.

On a lagoon-like section where the Calder is bisected by greenery, coots and moorhens poke weedy waters for invertebrates or fish, or peck at leaves, seeds or eggs. A paddling heron will drop its beak like a guillotine, or sweep into flight, a prehistoric-looking form conflicting with a backdrop of suburban houses.

Beside this slice of river is a wildflower paradise, thick with grasses: floppy daisies massing near water; yellow turnip weeds protruding from undergrowth like miniature maypoles; ragwort, whose feathery yellow florets are beloved by butterflies. The corridor was designed as a wetland habitat, but these drained soils suit dry-loving plants – sorrel and yarrow nestle amid yellow carpets of lady's bedstraw.

Further in amongst the flowers, more invertebrates emerge – bees and wasps, ladybirds, gummy-looking bloodsucker beetles. Cinnabar moth caterpillars, rich twists of black and orange, bend round stems. Grasshoppery potato capsids weave through teasel. From time to time, a longhorn beetle will flex its blue and white antennae, the length of which exceeds the beetle's body.

The road towards Sowerby Bridge takes in pond-like bodies of water, flanked by teasel, daisies almost as wide as hands, bindweed looming like snow-white moons.

Back towards the main body of the reserve, plant life is fading this late in summer, but in June the scene is like a lilac sea, riverbank glistening with thistles, teasel, buddleia, pink-ish pagodas of loosestrife, red campion patching the gaps. Like hairstyles of extrovert punk rockers, thistles mass by the roadside, adding the finishing touches to this purple reign. An orangey butterfly lands on a sun-silked flower head, yet within a moment takes flight once again, swerving on a puff of summer wind, disappearing among a sea of greenery.

In winter, I've watched the Calder almost burst its banks here. But on calm afternoons, the river rambles towards Copley, sunlight reflecting on its surface. Sometimes Canada geese pose on the weir – or a heron, all but camouflaged against the tumbling froth of the flowing Calder.

Planning the site, Calderdale council invited Wakefield-based CF Landscape to design the reserve, who pledged a 'holistic approach' recognising biodiversity. Given the thriv-ing wildlife seen all year along this beautiful reserve, it's fair to say this objective was fulfilled. Copley Valley Green Corridor is a fantastic feature of our local countryside, and an example of how humans can bring good as well as harm to the natural world.

Herons

Walking along the canal one chilly, early autumn Sunday, I pass waddling throngs of ducks, watch a canal boat pass beneath a bridge, chugging through the dusk towards Sowerby Bridge.

Plodding towards Copley, I'm caught by the glare of a beady eye - black, rounded by sharp yellow, piercing, accusatory. Almost more sinister is the razor beak - angled, dagger-like, towards the water. Almost, but not quite - because for all their predatory glower, there is something of the jester in a heron. Their flappy flights, legs a-dangle, can have a clumsy quality; the jutting neck can give the appearance of some odd, mechanical dance. Grey herons (*Ardea cinerea*) are suited to the watery Calder Valley. I see them sweep through sunsets, wings outstretched, an ashy pterodactyl above the roofs and tree-tops. At Barkisland, I watch them, semi-visible in fields of reeds, stationery under driving rain, outside Brearley, on the prowl for voles or shrews, or combing plumages with "grooming claws." You can see them fishing in the river, stock-still before the sudden plunge of a lethal beak, and the gobbling and gulping of large, fat fish. Occasionally, you might see a mother silhouetted against the bough of a tree, craning her neck, dispatching breakfast to her chicks.

Urban herons are not unheard of, though I've never seen one on the streets - the closest they have come was during the first 2020 Lockdown. Emboldened by our scarcer numbers, herons, like other birds, emerged for longer periods, on canal paths and on the edges of car parks, even residential areas. I saw one most days that spring, along the canalside, by the normally busy Wharf Street, and sometimes followed it, prodding around locks and milestones like some avian investigator.

Those surreal spring evenings, it felt like the birds were the natural citizens of the towpaths. Gone, for a few quieter, less polluted weeks, the cans, the cigarette butts and the fishermen, replaced by growing numbers of increasingly confident birds – an eco-system thriving without human influence.

The return to normal life has seen a gradual withdrawal of herons, back into semi-secrecy. I miss seeing them just a few yards away, eyeing me as if asking what brings me to their territory. They still appear, though, at further distances along a path, or waiting in water for fish, amphibians or eggs, watching with a hint of distrust as you pass by the canal.

Herons are contradictory birds: elegant predators, yet gangly and grumpy-faced; popular, yet a bit mysterious; gauche, conspicuous birds, not seen every day, yet instantly recognisable, and familiar as friends.

Swallows

Up on the telegraph wires over Norland Moor, the swallows are preparing to migrate, their blue tail feathers and inky wings dark against the cloudy sky.

Swallows – *Hirundo rustica* – are a frequent sight in the Calder Valley. I see them darting up into the eaves above my home overlooking the canal, which they skim on summer evenings in constant flight, hunting for insects. I see them up on the moors, on the outskirts of farms, dipping in and out of grasses. They live mostly on the wing, snaffling invertebrates, nesting in cool, dark, quiet sites like barns and unused farm buildings.

Swallows are distinguished from swifts or martins by, among other qualities, their size and the extremity of their forked tails. A swallow's head is dark around the eyes, but russety red about the beak, like a fiery face mask. Their song is cheepy and insistent, with three main sounds – a chirp, a gurgling sound and a plaintive moan – which are heard throughout the warmer months. Even a single swallow can provide glorious cacophonies of twitterings and trills, so distinctive that they can sound more like a musical instrument than a small bird. On these evenings of half-light, I sometimes stand below the telegraph wire halfway down from the moor, my ears enlivened by their song.

But now, as autumn nights draw in, these shimmering symbols of English summertime are about to bid our shores farewell. They will be maximising their insect intake, putting on the weight they need to sustain them through the migrations on which they are preparing to embark – their annual, incredible, cross-continental journeys.

Our summer guests will depart in large flocks, covering around two hundred miles a day, as fast as thirty-five miles per hour, flying low to conserve energy and often enduring long periods of scarce food. They will fly over France, across the Pyrenees, through eastern Spain and into North Africa. Some head across the Sahara or the Nile Valley. Others continue south or west, along the coast. All are aiming for the winter warmth of southern Africa.

The swallows are not alone in their migrations. We don't see many yellow wagtails in the Calder Valley, but those we do see along the river, stopping on rocks and weirs, will soon also be taking up a sea-bound course, as will willow warblers, swifts and turtle doves.

House martins are not unheard of in these parts, but they, too, will spread their wings and leave in the coming weeks, absent until March or April at the earliest. I first watched sand martins at Mixenden reservoir on a wet October evening several years ago – looping and swooping round the water's edges like black-and-white boomerangs, curved wings outstretched and piercing the autumn mists in knife-like arcs. The birds wove in and out of the sandy banks, where they nest, and circled the trees as if in preparation for the great departures they, too, would soon be making.

Very soon, these birds will no longer be seen on my afternoon walks, their claws pinning them to telegraph wires, or brushing the surface of the canal in their insect-searching twilight ballets. It is worth making the most of every sighting now, before they whisk themselves away to the warm climes of sub-Saharan Africa, thousands of miles from the reservoirs and cold moorland hills of the Calder Valley, until they return again in spring.

Back to Basics

The canalside walks around Sowerby Bridge and Halifax are courses I often tread, not least on these early autumn afternoons. They are bracing stretches, towpaths hosting the last stragglings of ragwort, meadowsweet and toadflax, the canal reflecting greens and yellows from the overhanging trees.

One of the best things about these waterside walks is the bird life: herons, cormorants, geese. As we head towards winter, glassy grebes will spool the water with unhurried elegance. Occasionally, I glimpse finches, jays or thrushes delving through the trees and bushes, nuthatches and treecreepers scarpering up trunks. At Salterhebble, blue tits hug the birdfeeders; outside Elland, swans drift by like slips of sailing chiffon. But I'd like to focus for a moment on some less celebrated canalside characters – ducks.

Few would regard mallards as exotic birds – yet if they were not so ubiquitous, they would surely be seen as rather fancy: the iridescent green faces of drakes, the females' marbled brown breasts and the blue swishes of the feathers are so often ignored.

I like to watch them perched by water, females gazing ponderously ahead, eyes like tiny black planets. They have a pensive, patient look, dignified and gentle, feathers speckled golden brown, lightly glazed in autumn sun. Drakes' heads are like sheeny green globes, especially when beaded with water. Their tail feathers twist into quiffs. Both sexes possess thick yellow beaks, which they swipe back and forth in elaborate self-grooming rituals as they clean their plumage.

Mallards are dabblers, taking most food at surface level. From time to time, they push their heads below the surface, but they are more typically seen cruising the canal, unfazed and calm, or waddling along wharfs, clambering over ropes or sunning themselves by the water's edge, occasionally erupting into cacophonies of quacks.

Hybrid ducks grace the canal, too. Recent regulars include a dark-feathered female whose colouring is whitened only in the large neck ring. She gave birth to a clutch of chicks this spring. There is also a mid-sized male with a mostly light brown body, but whose head, neck and tail feathers are a shade of racing green, and there are other birds of pebble-white, ruffly brown, coffee black.

Far from being overshadowed by geese, herons and more, our everyday ducks deserve more recognition. To watch as one unfurls its wings, mid-groom, is like seeing an aquatic ballerina, stylish and exquisite. At this time of year, in the absence of their migratory peers, mallards and their hybrid cousins take centre stage, and it is well worth our while giving these enduring, interesting, surprisingly beautiful birds their own moments in the spotlight.

Bleak Hinterlands

Up on Norland Moor these cool, crisp mornings, meadow pipits flit above browning grass. Late caterpillars curl in frosty pockets of foliage. Cobwebs bangle the grass, glistening in ice-like dew. The hills are blushing with heather, along with arrays of lemony gorse, gold dust in the morning sun.

Moorland is widespread across the Calder Valley, and rich in acid soils, hence the heathers, whose growing tips form parts of the diets of various birds. Kestrels, hovering in readiness for prey, swallows, sand martins and willow warblers have all winged their way into my sights upon the moorland hills.

One summer day on moorland near Lumb Bank, I watched a weasel weaving in and out of drystone walls; some miles east, this New Year's Day, a fox strolled by a moorland farm.

On a cold autumn afternoon eight years ago, I found a stoat stealing by a gate on the fringes of Norland Moor. Another autumn, on the margins of remote farms and woodlands, I noticed the soft shadows of two deer, moving slowly, like velvet silhouettes in morning mist.

The moors in autumn can be bright, inviting places, too. I've sat on piles of stones at Blackstone Edge, watching sun-washed moorgrass swaying like waves of golden sea. But autumn moorlands can also be chill, blustery environments, whose inhabitants are accordingly hardy: sheep that survive on tufts of grass; goats patrolling the bald, exposed hills; deceptively soft mosses hugging stony ground like sponges; red fungi, disc-shaped edges chewed by insects, growing in unlikely spots.

Outside Todmorden, the moors are defined by hilly dips, chunks of rock and ruined barns. The slopes above Mankinholes are riddled with old bones, skeletons and skulls of sheep sticking out of desolate earth, wind gusting over boulders.

For many, these bleak hinterlands spell danger, their altitudes guaranteeing extreme weather. On the moors at Ovenden and Warley, peaty earth stabbed with old standing stones, the wind hammers through crumbled remains of sheepfolds, howling and thrashing the angry edges of the reservoir. The paths and tracks of these remote spots, criss-crossing through rusty grass, are less trodden, their lumpy hills and jumbled rocks clambered up and down by hooves, or swooped above by hungry hawks, but rarely traversed by human feet.

But this rugged landscape, its beating winds and battered fences, its rough and bumpy terrain, stone barns and wary-eyed sheep, is as much the Calder Valley as the river and canals. With their sparse, skeletal trees, bare branches shuddering in the rain and wind, their shy birds dipping and diving over moss and bog, and their high, panoramic views over the distant lights of far-off towns, the moors of our district are fundamental to its character, and, at this time of year, ablaze in gorse and heather, autumnal jewels in the Calder Valley crown.

Autumn Leaves

Below my window, the canal trembles under pin pricks of rain. No ducks or geese pass by this autumn afternoon, only the occasional dog walker troops through the drizzle, along a towpath smudged in churned-up mud. But despite the chill of this dreary day, and the sullen sea of slate-grey cloud looming above in cold, foreboding gloom, the long stretch of the canal is full of colour. Light flickers with the shadows of reflected trees. Ripples spread like bars of melting metal, a bronzy ballet of autumn leaves.

Blackthorn, beech and ash leaves sail like slivers of burnt amethyst. They speckle the water in ochre ovals, or slender yellow arrows quivering in the breeze. Large, palmate leaves of sycamores hover like hands of autumn scarecrows, crisp and browning. In places, the winkling of chocolatey conkers is indistinguishable from the pot-pourri of nutty brown leaves piling up beside walls and hedgerows.

All over the valley, autumn leaves are carpeting parks and pavements, rouging roadsides and draping woodland floors in crêpes of crinkled copper. On the edges of Halifax town centre, or the towpaths snaking through Todmorden or Walsden, the ground beneath our feet is alive with fiery foliage – birch leaves, curled like veiny flames, those of the cherry tree fluttering to earth in flakes of red and amber. By the Calder at Sowerby Bridge, the tawny tears of the weeping willow seep from tree to water in a golden poetry of deciduous decrease.

Autumn Leaves

The next day, and I'm watching a houseboat cruising by before my window, splaying leaves in its wake like shoals of multi-coloured fish. Above, treetops glisten in a bounteous expanse – pigeons wobble on twigs hung with wine-dark leaves, a jay bobs through canopies of gingery brown, flashes of blue feathers vivid against dark branches. Swimming through leaves, a ruddy-feathered duck meanders by.

A couple pass along the towpath, matted like a rug of mottly maroons. A stray hazel leaf wafts down, settling amid the lanes of leaves dressing waters in a glaze of gold, like a slice of lemon in a goblet of rich whisky. The grey skies are slowly slit by the vein-like rays of a bloody sun, lacquering the valley in a resplendent blaze of autumn glory.

People's Park

Outside People's Park in Halifax, bushes are bulging with buckthorn berries, satsuma-orange. Around the fringes of this large park, the ground is plastered in slippery brown leaves, slick after the rain. Pretty and popular in summer, People's Park has much to offer in the later months too, and it provides a splendid showcase of quiet autumn colour.

Nestling between the terraced streets of King Cross, People's Park was created in 1857, given to the people of Halifax by Sir Francis Crossley, manufacturer, philanthropist and Liberal politician. On a visit to the White Mountains in New Hampshire, Crossley decided to recreate a microcosm of the area's impressive scenery in Halifax, "to arrange art and nature so that they shall be within the walk of every working man in Halifax; that he shall go to take his stroll there after he has done his hard day's toil, and be able to get home without being tired." Designed by Joseph Paxton and his assistant Edward Milner, People's Park has served the local population well ever since, and, complete with its elegant bandstand, flowerbeds and pond, it is a quiet oasis just a stone's throw from Halifax town centre.

At the western edge, stone statues are weathered in faded grandeur. Trees stand high, ash leaves hanging like wrinkly fingers. Flowerbeds still shine in soft colours – yellow rudbeckias curling and fading, anemones shining like snowflakes with gold stamens – and are bordered by sedum, purplish as autumn sunsets.

But while the floral features are the stuff of planning, this urban green space is also a boon for nature. In summer, flowers hum with bees and butterflies, bushes rustle with busy rodents, hungry thrushes comb the grass for worms.

In autumn, wildlife is scarcer, though occasional blackbirds tread twigs or plod through puddles, and the shallow waters are home to ducks that perform their grooming quite untroubled by walkers, picnicking families and playing children.

Sometimes, a crafty rat will dart from bank to water, snaffling grass or sprinting along the stone lip of the pond. Last November, I watched two racing in elaborate, dance-like rivalry to grab the fruits or insects that make up much of their diets. Eventually, one vanished into overgrowth, emerging moments later from a distant flowerbed, like a burglar caught in the act. The other slipped subtly into the water, paddling to the opposite bank and diving under cover of holly.

Beyond the Japanese-style bridge above the pond, pigeons amble over sandy banks, or tread the branches arched over the water like blue baubles.

A walk in the park may not seem an obvious pastime for a chilly autumn afternoon, and in a region rich with wild places it is easy to overlook more conventional sites for nature spotting. But the charms of People's Park cannot be overstated, and it is one of many Calder Valley parks well worth a visit not only in the warmer months, but now also, when the flowers may be fading but the birds still sing, and the trees glimmer softly in the russet of autumn.

Kingfishers

Like tiny comets, kingfishers zip over rivers and canals in search of fish and aquatic insects. Moderately populous – there are between 3,800 and 6,400 pairs in Britain – their speed and shyness nonetheless lend a sense of rarity to these glittery birds, giving their appearances a special, cameo quality.

Kingfishers, with sapphire wings and vivid orange under-parts, are no strangers to the Calder Valley, and might be glimpsed over any stretch of water bordered by low-hanging trees or bushes. I've watched from my window as they swoop over the canal at Sowerby Bridge, dipping over stony shallows where the Ryburn bubbles into the Calder, diving towards the banks, where they tunnel their unlined nests in cavities.

I've also seen them further along the canal towards Elland or Brighouse, azure arrows shooting by so fast that all one can discern are spangly sparks, scattering like luminous confetti through the rain. Only once have I seen one perched on a branch, poised above the Calder outside Ravensthorpe, pondering potential prey like a patient picaroon, cloaked in wings of lucent blue.

Preferring still or slow-moving water, kingfishers are not exclusively partial to rural or urban environments: one June afternoon, I watched a kingfisher swerve the rocky riverside in Dixie Wood, dancing its silent blue ballet into a weave of willowherb and Himalayan balsam. Yet I have seen them closer to town, also: crossing the bridge over the rain-beaten Calder on an afternoon heaving with traffic, I watched as silvery drifts of rain were slit by a thin blue blade, skimming the river's surface like a shooting star.

Kingfishers are vulnerable to habitat degradation and pollution, but in recent decades heightened water quality, and enhancement of Britain's canal network, have encouraged a reversal of their earlier decline, with reductions even in winter mortality rates.

Instantly recognisable, these birds are elusive gems: strolling by the river or any of the canal towpaths snaking along our valley on a summer's afternoon, you never can tell just when you might catch sight of one. Suddenly, the unmistakable blue wings and bronze breast fly into view for a matter of seconds only, before the bird bobs and swivels into overgrowth – just as quickly out of view.

Flying the Festive Flag

As snow fell over Calderdale in the last days of November, I noticed more and more berries around Halifax and Sowerby Bridge: the viscid globes of *Viscus album* – better known as mistletoe – whose opalescent balls will adorn branches between now and Christmas. Their presence is a sure sign the festive season is on its way. Indeed, at this chilly year's-end, hedges and trees are bursting with berries: firethorn hanging high; the sherry-red spheres of rowan; bright holly berries aglint against green leaves, enwrapped by swirling snow.

In the Brontë Garden at Sowerby Bridge station, I watched a blackbird peck for berries through the snow, a mistle thrush – named after its appetite for those waxy fruits – browsing the ground, sparrows and blue tits tiptoeing branches to attack bird feeders. But it is another festive favourite that has been most prominent: popping up in streetside hedges, in and out of trees, peppering the snow with its well-recognised breast of orangey red.

The robin redbreast – *Erithacus rubecula* – is synonymous with Christmas and seems more prominent than usual in winter, thanks not only to the contrast of its russet colouring with dark branches, but also to its habit of leaving the nesting area to investigate its surroundings in the colder months. It is in winter that both males and females sing, their trills Christmas courting songs.

Robins nest in an ingenious variety of environments, from obvious locations such as hollows, tree roots, logs and climbing plants, to unlikelier sites like discarded machines, barbecues, bike handlebars, upturned brooms, watering cans, hats and flowerpots. You will see them across all corners of the valley, from suburban gardens to moorland edges. At Cromwell Bottom, Brighouse, I watched a shaggy, scraggy juvenile twitching about a bird table, hoovering up scraps, its dishevelled feathers a bundle of browns and reds.

One freezing February day I watched a confident adult flitting through the woods at Ogden Water, its breast a festive red brightening winter dusk, and was amazed at just how long it posed on a fence, seeming to enjoy its moment in the spotlight of my camera. Up in the hills of Heptonstall, I watched a robin prepare for flight, poised briefly before taking off and shooting over fields and farmlands.

Heading into December, the snows have melted, and my local streets of Sowerby Bridge are lashed by rain. If forecasts are to be believed, the white stuff may yet return before Christmas, but whether it does or not, we can be sure that, like the holly and the mistletoe, as autumn stiffens into winter, the reliable robin will continue to visit our flowerbeds, feeders and gardens, flying the festive flag.

Boxing Day Deer

On Boxing Days, I'm often found wandering through wilderness quite a distance from home, the ground beneath my feet more than likely blanketed by snow.

It's odd to recall, amid this wintry wonderland, the summer afternoon in 2015 when I saw a mouse-like creature near the route of my Boxing Day walk the previous year: a shrew. I recall it whenever I cross that borderland between low-lying farms and paths straggling down from the moors. Shrews are less active in winter, their staple diets of spiders, slugs, amphibians and worms in shorter supply, so I'm less likely to spy one in the cold December snow, but this never stops me keeping an eye out for a small bundle of brown fur.

The patch of land I'm walking today is a magnet for wildlife. In the fields punctuated with sheep, where a lop-sided tree, partly uprooted, testifies to the wreckage of the recent Storm Arwen, I've seen rabbits in spring, bouncing out from hedgerows. Up on the moorland's fringe, I've watched a stoat burrow through bowers of towering grass, heard yowls of foxes echoing through winter midnights.

Today, I notice a roe deer at the field's far end, stock-still and gazing into the snowy distance. Anyone who has seen wild deer will recognise the startled eyes as the animal stops short, regarding its observer with something of the child's anxious curiosity. Deer are not uncommon in the Calder Valley, benefitting from the woods and open grassland, and I often see them in winter. This deer, standing shyly by a fence, is a dainty doe, coat already showing early touches of the red that will colour it in spring and summer.

I'm stationary, a hundred yards or so from the doe. Once sure that I pose no threat, she moves. She's slow at first; like some fairy-tale unicorn she sweeps through snow, burnished against chalk white, before picking up pace, springing over snow, forelegs tucked back, switching directions and spurting back towards the fence, continuing this athletic dance for some minutes, seemingly for sheer exhilaration.

As I head up the cobbles towards the moor, the deer is still intermittently visible – an ear here, a hoof there – as she canters past the walls and bushes bracketing the field from an all-but-frozen stream. But eventually, my glances fail to find her. All that is seen now is a wide expanse of snow, and the rickety fingers of bare trees, hanging above in thin black tapestries, as if the winter deer had been a dream.

A Year of Surprises

I'm looking from my window onto the Rochdale Canal, watching a mallard pass amid ripples. The towpath is puddled after rain, nearby cars carapaced in frost. The canal shivers beneath skeletal branches and doomy skies.

But recent snows, together with dramatic skies and colourful birds and berries, remind us that winter heralds beauties of its own. Every day I watch goosanders comb the cold canal, males with gleaming heads of green, females eagle-eyed with snow-white breasts and ginger tufts. Though year-round residents, they come into their own in winter, sliding with a cool finesse, like flakes of ice. Geese, like ruffled bundles of fresh snow, paddle frosts, or gaze across the water, their beaks beaded with sleet.

In uncertain times, the natural world has provided some stability. Against the backdrop of a continuing pandemic, nature has persisted and endured. I have felt greatly this year the influence of my own mother, who died in February. Her love for the wild world inspired my own.

It has been a year of first sightings – butterbur in early April, bunched by the towpath like little pink poles; the flecked brown female mandarin duck bobbing along the Ryburn one autumn afternoon – and old favourites, too: leggy herons sweeping over ponds; kingfishers swooping down the Calder; wild red roses trellising moorland edges; up on the tops, the freedom of fresh autumnal air, wind whistling through heather and howling over rocks.

A Year of Surprises

I've enjoyed the lesser-loved novelties of nature: multitudinous invertebrates, such as red soldier beetles bending stems of grasses at Copley nature reserve; weevils the colour of cola; alder leaf beetles, tiny balls of jet; multicoloured molluscs; the frog leaping down my street, a lithe, elastic acrobat, pogoing through the rain.

I've been struck by fungi: from squishy crystal brains to acid-red toadstools; white bracket fungi chunked around decaying logs; King Alfred's cakes smirching tree trunks like black blisters; mushrooms small as fingernails, hooded by grass blades amid farmer's fields.

I'm thinking back to algae, filming the edges of Willow Hall Dam, in swirling patterns as beguiling as watercolours. I'm recalling my first sightings of slime moulds on the towpath trees and hidden in the barky undergrowth on the outskirts of a park, and the unique spectacle of gummosis. I'm thinking of the gorse and heather up on the moors, erratic in its habits, having blazed in places through the early spring, and elsewhere exhibiting a frosty majesty as the autumn months drew in.

As the year draws to a close, I'm thinking back with gratitude on the diversity of wildlife that has graced our valley, taking comfort in the current cast of characters – the blackbirds, thrushes, gulls and grebes whose colours brighten winter trees and waters – and looking forward to the flora and fauna to come as we turn the page into a new year.

New Year Kestrels

Wandering the windswept fringes of Sowerby this New Year's Day, I find myself amid the stony lanes of Hubberton Green, whose fields are divided by a hotchpotch of drystone walls. Sheep graze the pale, yellowy grass, trundling towards feeding troughs, or gazing into wintry distances, where snowy clouds are scraped by leafless trees.

Stopping for a breather, I notice a downy frame poised on top of a telegraph pole around thirty metres away. Closer focus of the camera lens confirms it is a kestrel.

Like most falcons, the common kestrel – *Falco tinnunculus* – has long wings and tail feathers. It is widespread across much of the northern hemisphere. I see kestrels mostly on moorland above Sowerby Bridge or on the outskirts of Warley, swooping hillsides, or hanging in mid-air, as if flying on the spot, twenty metres or so above the ground.

The Woodland Trust's website describes a kestrel's eyesight as being so razor-sharp that the birds can spot a beetle fifty metres away. They can see ultraviolet light, enabling them to follow the urine trails of rodents. When prey is spotted, it is seized in a momentary dive. When young arrive in spring, females tear the spoils into manageable chunks for the two or three chicks that share the nest.

This kestrel, whose light, sandy plumage suggests is female, remains on the pole for some time, as if weighing up the world around her, before slighting with a swerve over through the trees and chimneys of a nearby farm, diving into dark clouds and the intricate camouflage of serpentine branches.

Birds of prey always seem unexpected to me, even in the heathy, shrubby moorland habitats where they are not uncommon, and hawks, with their evocations of pageantry, conjure something of the mediaeval to my mind. Indeed, those beige wings, folded like a tunic around the kestrel's back, chestnut-brown and chequered in black spots, lend it the look of a harlequin. It's a magical, mysterious bird, entertaining us with its dance before a split-second vanishing act.

But it is only a matter of days before my next sighting, another female, this time outside Copley.

The kestrel sits halfway up a leafless tree and as I edge closer she seems undisturbed, surveying the landscape with a downward gaze. A few steps further and my luck is out – the bird lifts off the branch towards another tree. Then she drops suddenly, landing with a thwack beside the hedge, before disappearing into the bushes bordering the viaduct.

But she will not be the last kestrel I spy in these parts, and in any grassy, rodent-rich habitat, on woodland edges, up on the moors, or out among the winding country lanes, I'll be keeping half an eye raised to the sky, just in case.

Fox Song

On winter nights, I've heard them – thin, ghoulish croaks, not so piercing as the howling of a wolf, but more mournful than the song of any bird. Without the cushion of vegetation, a fox's screams are heard more clearly. They are the sound of claiming territory: in the night, foxes call out to attract mates, and vixens will emit loud yowls during mating.

While it isn't unusual to hear their haunting cries rebound through moonlit woods or darkened streets, the sight of a fox is rarer, day or night; though I think, over the years, I've seen more in urban than in rural areas, prowling down deserted streets, disappearing into alleyways. But I've seen them in greener environs, too – sauntering through gardens, plunging into woodland undergrowth. Yesterday, while walking through open fields somewhere between Mytholmroyd and Cragg Vale, I watched a fox trot over a drystone wall, then slip through the grass in a flash of red.

Elusive, mysterious, somehow simultaneously familiar and mysterious, carrying in the swoosh of their sinuous bodies a flame of mediaeval England, foxes are animals of the margin – the dimly lit edges of our towns and cities, the fringes of fields and lonely stretches of canal towpaths, in and out of boscage, half insouciant, half evasive.

Slinking through my moonlit street late on bitter-cold nights, foxes remind us of a parallel, non-human nocturnal world, while their distant cries punctuate the early hours with dark, elemental winter poems.

Cormorants

Sometimes on a morning as I walk over the bridge, I see a cormorant by the Calder, poised on a log, beak aimed at the sunrise, like an early-rising pirate.

There is something primeval about cormorants. I watch as they haunt the riverside on the outskirts of Sowerby Bridge, or perch on rusty railings. Spreadeagled, wings outstretched, they seem to resemble huge prehistoric bats – around a metre in length from beak to tail. As the RSPB points out, a cormorant's lengthy neck lends a reptilian element to their appearance. Distinctive, with black feathers and slightly chunky beaks, they are mistaken only for the similarly sized and coloured shags, although cormorants have white patches around the face, and sometimes elsewhere. There are around 40,000 cormorants in Britain, with a significant wintering population.

When I see cormorants locally, they are almost always stock-still and solitary. They nest in colonies, though, and I've watched them in twos and threes in reservoirs and ponds further afield. They favour lagoons, rocky shores and estuaries, but here in the valley it is the river that seems to lure them, with its regular supplies of fish – making up the majority of their diet – and its banks, where their messy nests are twined in the vegetation.

Along with dawn sightings, I've seen cormorants on late afternoons, meditative sentinels in the drizzly grey. Sometimes they seem to prefer the darkened margins of the river, where they merge into the shadows. Other times, they will pose on stones in the centre of the water, brooding, unmoving, like silent obsidian sphinxes.

It is often said that cormorant wings are not waterproof, but this is not strictly so. Like most birds, cormorants secrete a glandular oil with water-resistant properties, but not in sufficient volume to provide full protection. The structure of their feathers also renders them 'wettable' – reducing buoyancy to enable deeper dives – which is why cormorants are often seen spreading their wings to dry them. The action also helps the feathers realign and absorb heat in sunshine and assists with balance and parasite removal. Even though cormorants spend a lot of time in water, it is in this statuesque pose that we most often see them, and how I have come to expect cormorants: totemic and inert, unfurling long, tapered wings.

Later in the day, cormorants are harder to discern, but from the same bridge above the river I've still made out their immobile black bodies in the fading light. Or, irresistibly eerie, they will sweep downstream, then submerge themselves below the surface, before flapping up into a silent glide, bending through the dusk like thin black boomerangs, until their dark shapes dwindle into the distance, becoming one with the night.

Stormy Weather

Yesterday, hammered by Storm Eunice, parts of the valley saw trees uprooted and fences flattened. Having left early in the cold calm before the storm, I returned late, to heavy rain and a river bulging towards the top of its banks.

The morning after the storm, the Calder surged through Sowerby Bridge. A lone goosander slid along its course, propelled by the current. Yards away, the canal towpath was almost eerily serene, shady corners coated with snowdrops, whose petals were not yet fully open.

On Norland Moor I see two fallen telegraph poles, neatly laid like bodies in a morgue – uprooted not by Eunice, but by November's less severe Storm Arwen. For weeks afterwards they could be seen, bent and twisted, leering over the icy pond. Now they lie filed by the moorland edge, dead wires tied about redundant fuses, a sign of how even the power of electricity can be cut down in a trice by the might of nature's blade.

Up on the moors this nippy Saturday, the weather is still blustery and sleety, but it is not tempestuous. The storm has died down, and as I cast my eyes across the horizon, the Calder Valley is dusted by a veneer of snow, thickening up on the moor tops. The ground crunches softly beneath my feet. Along the horizon, the roofs and red bricks of King Cross are white, church spires lifting like the beaks of Arctic birds. Towards Sowerby, and up into Warley, Mount Tabor and Jerusalem Farm, the hills are robed in snow, melting into seas of creamy cloud.

A Year in the Calder Valley

A few dog walkers dot the distance, and an over-excited pup performs a frenzied dance around my ankles. As I walk on, the moor is spongy underfoot. It is hard to believe that less than twenty-four hours earlier, a raging storm advanced across these hills, a scything cyclone ravaging branches and smashing through homes. Railway stations have been pummelled, lorries overturned. Three people have lost their lives.

Above, the sun shifts, sometimes behind and then again in front of the clouds, like a pearl wrapped in folds of silk, obscured and emerging once again with an icy brilliance. And now, the rain intensifies.

All through the evening, a tide of rain heaves in, pushing the canal and river ever more toward their limits. By night, it is lashing down with merciless force, the kind of rain that drenches jeans and seeps through shoes, wheedles its way into your bones – relentless, almost biblical.

Sunday begins mild and dry. My corner of the valley is enveloped in a picture-postcard calm, chocolate-box bucolic. Church bells peal, blackbirds chirp. All traces of the snow are gone. The violence of the storm is now simply a memory, washed out by the furious night rain, and thawed in the thin winter sun.

Walking by the canal, I search in vain for some metaphor with which to comprehend the changeability of the elements. I notice only the boats, the shapes of birds among the branches of denuded trees, and the tiny snowdrops with their finger-high stems still secure, having escaped the damage meted out by the storm to buildings and trees. They are joined by burgeoning crocuses, and the sheaths of daffodils, ranged along the bank like slim shafts of sunlight.

Stormy Weather

These few days seem proof of nature's power, its unpredictability, the transience of even its mightiest of moments. As I write on a dark February night, the media warn more storms could soon be on the way, as, exacerbated by human abuse, the planet warms and undergoes changes that increase the frequency of destructive weather events. But I am not a climatologist, nor an expert on the weather. I can only reflect on the ferocity and variation, and the glimmers of resilience encountered in this wild week, and on how, outside my window in the pitch-black night, the rain comes tumbling down, again.

Stoodley Pike

Buffeted by winter winds, I clunk through cloughs and boggy, soggy, swamp-like moors outside Todmorden, up to my ankles in mud. It is late February, and on this biting afternoon the far-off turbines are shawled in ribbons of mist. A pale sun drools icy light across the choppy waters of the reservoir.

No rain falls, but a week's-worth of downpours has left the ground a mushy mat. The desire paths tramped into the steep hills are slicked in slippery, wet moss.

It's a few years since I was last here, and I feel semi-lost in the quagmire, where every footstep seems to land in deeper water. I run into a jogger, much more sensibly kitted out in his water-proofs than I am in my drenched denim and torn cagoule. After he has given me directions, I watch him sink into the cloud-capped distance, until he has become a speck of blue Lycra, moving along the far-off ridges like a tiny, brilliant bird.

To the south, the sodden moors roll toward Manchester. The small former mill towns of east Lancashire lie to the west, while east is Cragg Vale, haunt of eighteenth-century counter-feiters, along with the tough, blackened terrain of moorlands. Ahead to the north is the dark-bricked, 120-foot Stoodley Pike monument, at the summit of the hill of the same name.

Completed in 1865 at the end of the Crimean War, the monument's history assumes an ironic poignancy against contemporary events, and trudging these rock-strewn, uphill miles, it's hard not to think of those on their inhospitable treks, not through choice but in fear for their lives.

Below, surrounded by fields sliced up by drystone walls, Todmorden is a grey smudge, dark hills rising from behind. Above this basin, the cloud is blotted by a yolky sun. Few birds fly, but there is the occasional sulky chuckle of a grouse, black forms whisking from the cover of one tangle of bushes to another.

Cone-shaped like a mediaeval witch's hat, the dark spike of the pike rises against purpling cloud. In its shadow, walkers and lone cyclists look like Lilliputian stick figures. The brown heather dwindles as I walk along, giving way to a thin mat of grass, which itself is eventually superseded by a chequerboard of large, uneven stones – jagged slabs and diamond-shaped, cobbled rocks.

To ascend the monument is to enter total darkness, hear the scraping of your shoe against brick steps, wind your way up a spiral of pitch-black, emerging on a wind-battered balcony, not even halfway up. Here, the wind is so remorseless that I have to literally hold on to my hat. It whistles and bashes against bricks scrawled in moss and yellow lichen. Above, the sun is setting, the horizon bleached by streaks of peachy pink. Below, a cyclist wheels into the enveloping embrace of a tree plantation, which swallows her up.

Around the bend of the balcony, a bearded and anoraked Spanish man is mapping out the landmarks in the distance to a woman standing with him. This way is Halifax, he says, pointing, and that way Manchester. A remote tower of flickering red lights is the tallest freestanding structure in the UK, Emley Moor transmitter, blurry lights like eyes of wary moorland mammals, distant, nebulous, almost morphing into the hibernal sunset.

A Year in the Calder Valley

Once alone, I pace the platform like a castle guard, resting my elbows on the slab of a sill, and gaze into space from this Pennine minaret. Below, the rough terrain bevels into hills, giving way to a tumbling plunge, 1,300 feet down towards Todmorden and beyond.

Ovenden Moor

It's been some years since I ventured up to Ovenden Moor, which lies on the valley's ragged edges. It hosts a fourteen-tower wind farm to the north of Halifax. Fresh from yesterday's hike to Stoodley Pike, this bleak borderland between Halifax and Bradford seems an apt destination for another winter-time wander.

The weather is bracing – brisk, and with a winter wind cutting through the air. Virtually everywhere in the Calder Valley is uphill, and the trek up Tuel Lane towards Warley is no exception. As I push on through the herringbone pattern of terraces, inspired by the poetic-sounding Milton Street, the hills of Norland and Copley lift behind me, above the roofs and chimneys of Sowerby Bridge, the forecourts of its super-markets, the old brick factories and their adjacent wastelands. The wind is punishing, the temperature plummets. The road seems to incline further. Not for nothing, I suppose – as I do every single time I pass it – is the road halfway up this inter-minable climb called Perseverance Street.

Wainhouse Tower is visible from the bend at Green Hill; to the south-west are the miles of moorland stretching above Sowerby Bridge and reaching out into Soyland, Ripponden and the motorway. I pass a half-built house, some horses in a field, and follow the road leading up into the village of Warley. The road names here are redolent with Yorkshire his-tory – natural and social: Workhouse Lane, Withens Road, South Clough Head, Cold Edge Road.

A Year in the Calder Valley

The sky spreads cerulean blue above the scattered houses, farms and pubs that punctuate the undulating expanse of Luddenden valley, spread below to the west. In the far centre, before a backdrop of darkened moor, is the old premises of Oats Royd Mill. Further on are dams and reservoirs, and on my right, incongruously, a children's playground, where a man and boy kick a football back and forth, a timeless ritual amid this almost primeval landscape of bald hills, trees curled above them like the fingers of demonic gods.

A strange suburbia seems to have sprung up from nowhere, and as I walk past semis and pebble-dash driveways, I begin to wonder whether I've taken a wrong turn. I just don't recognise this street of bungalows, garages and garden gates, with its parked cars and neatly parted curtains. I could be back in the Leeds suburbs of my youth, and I almost expect to hear the ditty of the old ice-cream van tinkling down the street, but for the gaping expanses on all sides. Soon, this slice of suburban domesticity peters out, usurped by fields and occasional snaky lanes, lonely cottages and sheep.

Up here, it is raw and frosty, with a smattering of snow on the other side of the drystone wall that separates this long, straight road from fields sloping to a reservoir. This latter is shaped like a big, ungainly puddle, and a number of sailing boats are moored to its banks, their sails looking incongruent against this windswept vista of frost-bitten February fields, trees flailed by heavy winds. A nearby crow stands stock-still in the grass.

Up ahead, the steel stalagmites of wind turbines slice through freezing air and loom over passing cyclists like robotic wicker men. On the edge of one marshy field, a sheep eyes me silently, standing like a woolly watchman, while stretched behind is one great, long blanket of bare, barren terrain, bleak against a horizon crowned by the distant turret of Stoodley Pike. Further on I trudge, past a panoply of plantations, farms and more endless fields. Then, a surprise – the unexpected, long-beaked form of a curlew, poised upon a drystone wall, gazing out towards the skyline.

The moor creeps up on you slowly, from behind a barbed wire fence, much of it initially hidden behind hills. It opens out slowly onto rumpled dunes of tough moor-grass, stony hillocks and occasional bare trees, a lunar lair of rutted paths and patches of bone-white snow, until, before long, a ramshackle stile is crossed, and you enter a cratered Sahara of sandy clefts, where hollows and rocks are jutting from the tussocks on every side.

In a basin of hills, I watch a fox moth caterpillar, a trickle of black and orange, gyrate across a slab of slate-coloured stone. Beside me, lacy slivers of ice rest on stalks of grass, like a necklace of tears. I wend my way past old stone structures – like Anglo-Saxon settlements, they are disused sheepfolds, or perhaps the barns of some long-ago farm. I try to imagine the lives of the hardy shepherds who might have trekked this bitter wilderness, the quarriers who hacked a living among these ruins. A grouse reels across the near distance, veering over the hill and reappearing, looping back above a declivity drenched in melting snow.

Once I have climbed – at times on hands and knees – above and beyond this opening frontier, I'm greeted by a barren-looking moor, cairns interspersed like pagan pikes, threadbare grass shining in the early evening sunlight. It's biting cold now, wind rasping over the boulders. Skies darkening, shafts of an insistent sun still appear through steeled clouds.

A few hundred yards away, up above on the brow of the hill, a tall figure and four children march through the sunset. Silhouetted in the dusk, hair waving in the breeze, they could be the Brontës exploring the moors. Indeed, the sunlit periphery of Thornton Moor and Haworth's wild edges can be seen to the north.

Red lights in the misty distance tell of small outlying towns, but out here you could be almost anywhere, miles from civilisation. To my east, the family on the hill fades into the twilight. When I turn around, I see that the whole backdrop of the moor behind me is now lit up in gold as a brilliant winter sun floods the sky in a glorious swansong of dying light.

Sunset at Warley Moor Reservoir

On the final day of February, fresh from my foray across Ovenden Moor, I press on towards the wide, marshy tract that is Warley Moor, with all its knolls and muddy pools hidden like elephant traps in the bumpy, swampy ground.

Squelching through the reeds, I trace the outline of a thin wooden fence, the beck-like trails of water draining from the reservoir, which was constructed between 1864 and 1872. A powdering of snow spreads across the ground, harsh white against the looming dusk.

By now it is bitterly cold, the twilight darkening, and the expanse of the reservoir sprawls like a sleeping beast, its edges lapped by waves that roll off the surface as if more out of habit than aggression.

'Beware,' says the wooden sign, planted firmly in the quagmire, 'Deep Mud.' But I see this warning a moment too late, as my foot is completely submerged in a quicksand-like clutch of hungry mud. Half of my leg soon follows. Slogging towards the drier edge of a reedbed where the grasses tremble in the evening breeze, I drag myself along a half-sunken wooden walkway, which sinks into the mud beneath my feet like the plank of an old pirate ship.

Just over a century ago, Halifax author Whiteley Turner traversed the same terrain, observing in his splendid book *A Spring-time Saunter round and about Brontë-land*: 'How shallow the water looks; so low that little islands of black heath protrude above its surface.' It doesn't look too different today, but after my muddy misadventure, I don't feel like taking my chances with the shallow waters. I do my best to stay as far as possible from the reservoir's edge.

In Turner's day, the area was also known as Fly Flatts, and described by the author as 'the bleakest of moorland' – an estimation not hard to echo on this blustery evening. Periodically, the weather grows rougher, wind whipping the reservoir's rim, sending sprays of ice-like water smacking against the shore, before the elements once again subside into a sort of freeze.

A red gloaming is setting in above, as the horizon slowly fades to pumpkin orange. The outline of the reservoir is sharpened in this lantern-like haze. 'We watch with interest a few black-headed gulls,' writes Whiteley Turner, who took to the scene with a telescope, 'a large family of which make Fly Flatts their habitation from year to year. Some basking in the sunshine, others, uttering a wailful note, are gracefully cleaving the air.' I see nothing of black-headed gulls, but a couple of Canada geese all but stroll across the water, which shimmers in the sunset in a rippling mixture of blue and rosy glows. Above, colours suffuse the banks of cloud.

With my camera in place of Turner's telescope, I aim towards the heavens, at a sun on fire; it is mirrored on the water by a huge, swelling ball of orange.

It is hard to find any sort of path as I tramp through miry miles of mud beneath a blooming burgundy sky, as the horizon begins to dip into darkness. High up on the main road, I run into two men who have pulled over to take photographs of the setting sun, its dramatic colours still illuminating the clouds, its molten orange exuding rays of red and yellow.

Sunset at Warley Moor Reservoir

Long afterwards – as I clomp the deserted road in the cold towards the oasis of electric light that represents a distant Sowerby Bridge – the moor and its reservoir, a squiggled shape of black glass, are kindled in a dusky sunset, and by the time the moorlands peter into paths and barns and narrow lanes, the sun itself is fading, a mizzle of cinders, sinking into starry blackness.

Winter Skies

This winter, our Calder Valley sky has been an ever-changing canvas of colour, from early mornings gently lit by sunrise seeping through the clouds, to the crimson light of winter sunsets, pools of purple staining the horizon like spilt wine. Nowhere has been a more ideal platform from which to view these sky light shows than the seat of a train. To slip into the lavender of a winter sunrise, with track-side fences fleeced in frost, is to be granted access to an artist's studio – like watching Monet or Kandinsky spatter their canvases in swirls of paint, sousing sky in impressionistic patterns.

The skies seem wider spread over open landscapes. The stretches of fields, river and canal, punctuated by houses or business parks between the valley's outlying towns, have been especially graced with beautiful skies. Early morning sun lights up the riverside and towpaths. It animates hedgerows so that the overwintering birds can be seen pecking through newly berried branches.

Outside Brighouse, I watch a deer bolt from the bushes, buffed in sunshine; downriver at Mirfield, the heron I spy most mornings as it perches beside the tumbling weir is lustred by sunlight like a dancer in the spotlight. At Ravensthorpe, the train swings past ponds and locks, the river widening below and stretched like a long blue belt, its waters burnished by the rising sun.

Journeys home, too, are a nightly spectacle, when the old town of Dewsbury is lit up in all its faded Victorian glory by soft sunlight. The civic spires, churches and the walls of the old shoddy and mungo mills are enlivened by rose-tinted skies.

As my train delves west, into the claret of a February sunset, the façades of former factories and the crumbled ruins of demolished buildings are illuminated as, above, plaited clouds, like a moonscape, are painted in pink. Throughout the journey home, the heavens burn with shades of the dying light, as the sunlight slowly fuses to magenta. Like rainbowy mazes of glassy agate, rays of the fading sun decorate the chimneys in tongues of flame, ribboning pylons like paper streamers.

Lately, shifting in and out of sleep, I watched through the train window at a yellowing welkin washed in the embers of an amber sky, as February drew to a close. Briefly, it seemed the entire horizon had been doused in liquid fire.

Walking the moors this time of year, night sets in quickly. There is a brief window of time when the skies seem tinctured in the mauves of sundown, pink as the petals of heather at your feet. Only recently, I saw a different kind of moorland sunset, up at Norland. A ghostly white disc of winter sun flickered in and out of vision behind thickening snow clouds. Soon, the whole panorama was fogged over by a sort of woolly light, slowly subsiding into nightfall.

Somehow even more spectacular than those of summer, the pyrotechnics of a winter sky are a wonder to behold. Perhaps the magic lies in the unleashing of light, as if, for those brief intervals of dawn and evening, the soul of summer has been let loose upon a frozen world. Perhaps there is something life-affirming, even in the brevity of its rise and fall, about the sun and its persistence, lighting a world of darkness.

From behind the safety of my window, I've looked up to a fiery firmament and felt drawn to the empyrean, as the canal below, the apartments beside the wharf, the old flues and fac-tories of Sowerby Bridge, and the long, climbing road up to Sowerby are all ignited by the light of a rose-robed sun.

On clear winter evenings, the far skyline's bare treetops are silhouetted against orange, as lines of Canada geese file into the sunset. This bonfire of the sky will burn until displaced by dark, replaced by the starry origami of night sky, and super-seded by the slate of the winter moon.

Crocii

Early March, and the crocuses again light up the entrance to Sowerby Bridge's Crow Wood Park, verges crackling with colour. Yellows, whites and violets are massed on the grass like constellations of confetti, petals brocading the roadside in soft, peaceful shades of spring.

Beside Halifax's Savile Park, the strips of grass by the road are adorned in bunches of white and purple. Even though these displays spring up every year, it is always slightly unexpected, and after a tumultuous twelve months there is a definite sense of reassurance at the sight of their familiar reappearance.

These crocuses are not wild; they are planted and maintained by the council. But their presence is greatly beneficial to wildlife. Not only are moths and beetles attracted to their rich stores of nectar, they are also visited by pollinating birds and early butterflies. On a cold but sunny March morning outside Crow Wood Park, I glimpsed my first bumblebee of the year, buzzing between clumps as if dizzy at the sheer numbers on offer. Just yesterday at Skircoat Green, I watched another bee diving in and out of flowerheads, rich with their newly minted pollen.

Crocuses are in the iris family, introduced to Britain by the Romans. There are around 200 species, and they provide a well-loved sign of spring in parks and on roadside verges nationwide. Wild crocuses can be found in small clusters on a walk along the canal towpath, or a lone crocus lifting from a bankside amongst dead wood and leaves, igniting the undergrowth in a tiny saffron sunrise. In Sowerby Bridge, the towpaths are brightened now by snowdrops, daffodils, primulas and crocuses.

Known as snow crocuses, some of the 'wild' varieties are garden escapees that have naturalised and spread. Their appearances are fleeting, their flowers smaller than those most commonly cultivated, Dutch crocuses. Another type is the early crocus – *Crocus tommasinianus* – flowering in February and March, and often seen carpeting parks in quilts of purple.

Whether naturalised or cultivated, crocuses are a highlight of the year. Be they on the edge of the canal, on the roadside at Bolton Brow, where their wash of soft colours lends a soothing respite to the driver or pedestrian overwhelmed by busy traffic, or, indeed, adorning the approaches of our parks and gardens, they mark the turn of the season as spring approaches.

I like winter, and delight in its many natural riches, but it seems to have been an extraordinarily long one this year. As the evenings grow lighter, and the birdsong of a morning seems longer and more plentiful, the emergence of the crocuses are cheerful reminders of renewal, and make a very welcome change.

Rabbits

Ploughing through fields of thickening green, our train is nearing the edges of Sowerby Bridge, where, this spring morning, sheep are grazing in sunshine, and the window is brushed by just the thinnest drizzle of April rain.

We don't get much sun in the Calder Valley, but the current bright spell hints at warmer times to come, at least for a while. Step outside on a light, mild morning, and you will notice increased numbers of birds – freckle-breasted mistle thrushes foraging in treetops, blue tits shifting branch to branch. On occasion, a jay flashes its cerulean sash through birch and oak boughs. The frosts have melted. Buds are bursting from the bushes. Roadsides are fringed with pink and golden wildflowers. It is springtime in the valley.

The train crosses the viaduct, past the widening river, over the hills above Copley, skirting the cricket club and the bend of the canal. The fields here are typical of the local landscape – sloping, bumpier than a classic farmer's field, bisected here and there by a fence or drystone wall. These demarcations look more as though they have been awkwardly fitted around the fields than as if they conformed to any regulated measurement.

This is farm country, for sure, but not farmland that is easy to manage or that will ever yield readily to the human hand. Here and there, a derelict shed is half covered by overgrown grass. A makeshift trough in the form of a rusty bathtub gathers dirt beside a pond. An antiquated tractor slumps beside the fence halfway up a hill, as if having admitted defeat.

This lumpy, uneven terrain seems best suited to sheep. I watch them cramming the grasses by a dirt track and huddling around a pylon in the centre of a field. And around the upper edges of this fleecy scene I see small, mousey-brown shapes in the grass, or darting into hedges or the cover of trees. These rabbits are my first of the year. The more I look, the more seem to appear.

There is something I find quietly triumphant about the sight of these shy creatures reappearing after the cold of winter. Recent evidence suggests they may originally have been brought here by the Romans as pets. But to me, the sight of rabbits nibbling grass seems nonetheless to conjure the essence of an English spring.

Weeping Willows

Sowerby Bridge is blessed with illustrious weeping willows, and the wider Calder Valley hosts many more of these beautiful trees. With pendulous branches sleeved in spirals of arrowy green leaves, weeping willows – *Salix babylonica* – originated in China, but they have adorned British parks, watersides and streets for many years.

Entering Sowerby Bridge at Bolton Brow, you will be greeted by a tall, sprawling willow spilling its foliage over a roadside garden. Further down in the town, another stands bright against the white walls of the Royal Lofts apartments, an umbrella of lime green transforming a drab car park and adding a touch of glamour to an otherwise largely leafless corner.

Further afield, at Copley, a willow graces a neat suburban street. Along the towpath at Salterhebble, another hangs by the bridge, blue tits flitting in and out of its leaves every spring. My favourite willow is at Mytholmroyd: this tree cloaks the canal in splendid springtime colour. On warm evenings I love to see its mirror image shining on the water, in reflected sunlit pools of lush sea-green.

In late winter, willows present hopeful touches of green against backdrops of grey, although they are often checked by snows. Only weeks ago, I watched March snows settle on the branches of a weeping willow.

That particular tree is the one I always see en route to the station, on a shady lane along the Calder's banks, at the edge of a trading estate. In early spring, this growth contrasts with its less leafy neighbours, a solitary frazzle of refreshing green, leaves draped over the river like the tassels of a fancy dress. Now, in April, its leaves are gradually unfurling in elegant gleams, long green tongues touching the river in delectable reflections.

Weeping willows will bloom until midsummer, scattering catkins, curled and furred and bright with pollen, like snazzy caterpillars. Recently I seem to have come upon them every day – willows overhanging bodies of water, like my canal-combing favourite at Mytholmroyd, casting wavy green reflections on the catkin-cluttered surface, or adding dashes of colour to the concrete backdrops of dull car parks.

I'm noticing willow trees I have never noticed before, looking out for them on trains. With their cascading growth habits providing cover for insects, and heavily nectarous flowers attracting butterflies, bees, moths and many more beneficial insects, willows are among the area's stand-out trees, and are at their resplendent best in spring, brightening roadsides and flourishing by the river, their reflections rippling on the water.

April Showers

Let's face it, the Calder Valley is an excessively wet and rainy place. By the end of my first summer in Sowerby Bridge, I was coming to the realisation that a few days without showers was more unusual than a straight week of wet weather – and that, were I to remain resident in these pluvial parts, I would simply have to learn to love the rain.

The onset of spring is no bulwark against wet weather here, and the old adage of 'March winds and April showers' holds true – except that there are plenty of showers in March, too. Since moving to the valley about a decade ago, I've witnessed rainfall and flooding of historic proportions – the Boxing Day Floods of 2015 stand out most in local memory, but other years saw their own share of excess, too. Soaking winters, stormy summers, autumns dripping with continual downpours – there is rarely a cease to the rain's insistence in this valley, known as a "drainage basin" in geographical terms.

But there is something very distinctive about spring rain. Something precipitous about its start – sensed before felt – something reassuring, as if we haven't hurtled head-first into a new season and lost all traces of the old; something rather sweet about the way the skies heave with clouds that split to relieve the stuffiness of humidity with rain, freshening the air.

On many an April afternoon, I've sat by my window watching waves of driving rain sweep through the trees, and this year has been no exception. Nor have my outdoor wanders been free of it. Up on Norland Moor, I've felt the chilly fall of spring rain, pattering in single drops at first, then rushing down without relent on the heather, plashing on ponds, darkening the distant hills and villages in heavy grey surges, bending the trees and siling down on barns and standing stones.

Leaving home early one morning, I watched the rain from the cover of a train as we slid through Sowerby Bridge. Driving tides of water lashed hills in steely grey, smashing against the river's foaming eddies and carrying the Calder downstream in furious embrace. At Copley, the cricket pitch was all but waterlogged, and as we swung out towards Salterhebble, the rain teemed down in streams, billowing, washing out the fields.

In the early morning after a night of rain, there is often a silent, glacial beauty, especially in the tender days of early spring. Sunlight illuminates strands of cobwebs and pockets of dew. Walking the streets in town, I keep an eye out for cobwebs strung along wire fencing, jewelling the nooks and crannies of abandoned buildings like brocaded rainbows, bathed in tears of morning rain.

Slipping down the towpath by the canal, the ground is stuffed with tufts of willow catkin, wet bristles sparkling. Alongside, the path is bordered by gangly alders, walnut trees and ash, branches bangled in rainwater, canopies bent by magpies, shaking droplets from the dark green leaves.

Crow Morning

My front window faces onto the Calder and Hebble Navigation, a stretch of canal connecting Calderdale with Wakefield. This late in April, the birches opposite are now fully clothed in lime green gowns, while behind them the hills are grassy, sown here and there with sprinklings of white – flocks of sheep and newborn lambs, high up towards Norland Moor, like patches of unexpected snow.

Up among the hills, further bundles of trees bunch up in thick spring leaf. Below, the reflected foliage of hazel, birch and ash tinge the canal in a soft shade of green. A few stray leaves lie on the surface.

A large crow scoops itself up through the air before the window and onto the roof, a twig clenched in its mouth. Various birds nest up there, and many more among the trees below, where flashy jays and earthy brown thrushes dodge in and out of their canalside canopies on this cool morning.

Beside the water, one tree is still without leaves, and two dunnocks stab their way into its crown of spindly brown, scouting through a scaffolding of branches as, on the adjacent stone wall, an inquisitive crow prods his way above the banking.

The bank itself is fast becoming a thatch of greening bushes, hung with ivy threading snake-like towards the water. Hawthorn blooms, and bluebells flower. Over the tree-tops, three more crows lift at once, like a travelling flag of black draping the cream-coloured sky. Soon this dark trio disappears into an April morning that teeters on the edge of warmth, a twisting tattoo, singeing the pale blue. Birdsong rings out like church bells across the hills and echoes on the streets. and a sun the colour of orange juice widens in the sky like a waking smile.

Goslings

It was wonderful to see the new arrivals by the canal at Sowerby Bridge, as fluffy clusters of golden goslings munched and bumbled into view from mid-May onwards. I stumbled on them first one afternoon, the sunniest of the spring so far, five or six snuggled together half asleep or blinking into the daylight. These were young Canada geese – even though their feet were already wrinkled and leathery. Through slit-like eyes they glimpsed the world, in and out of sleep, under the watchful gaze of a proud, upright-standing mother goose.

It was a Sunday, and people milled by the waterside, taking photographs, responding as we might to the sight of newborn babies, an event that always brings out the child in us, too. Even though we know that they will come each year, there is a sense of relief, replenishment, on seeing these bundles of fluff, reminders of spring and foretellers of summer.

Later, I watched processions of goslings totter down the bank to test the water. Some began to swim, or nimbly tread water, before scurrying back to a cleft of soil and stones in the path. These canal-combing chicks muddled through muddy shallows and clambered up the bank, cheeping with excitement, picking their way past ducks and geese, exploring their environment with all the adventurousness of the young and naïve.

Closely guarded by wary parents, the goslings bobbed by the towpath, the feathers on their backs a slushy grey flecked with yellow, sunny-coloured heads nodding keenly as they hobbled along one by one, mimicking the nibbling and chomping of their elders.

Over the next few evenings, I saw them at different points along the path, sometimes tucked under the mother's wing, at other times toddling through the shallows or braving the wider waters of the canal with scrambling zest, like little fluffy suns, in their element.

Shibden Park

Famous as the home of landowner, gardener and diarist Anne Lister (as in the television series *Gentleman Jack),* the early fifteenth-century Shibden Hall stands amid acres of rolling hills and water, and makes a perfect sojourn for a spring afternoon.

I haven't visited Shibden since before the pandemic and, this bright May day, I'm surprised to rediscover how close it lies to Halifax town centre. Over the busy criss-crossing roads that brim the town to the top of a hilly pinnacle taking in Shibden Hall Road and Beacon Hill –and from where superb panoramic views of Halifax and the wider valley can be seen – you approach the park from its eastern edge, where it nestles in the heart of the Shibden Valley.

Through the bounteous gardens, I wander first in the beech woods, a cornucopia of wild garlic spangling the banks in satiny flowers caught by sunlight filtered through the shade. The terrain levels out at the garden's rampart-like walls, and a pond lies a stone's throw from the steps that lead to the hall.

The pond is festooned in purple lily pads and overhung with succulent foliage. The cheeping of a coot can be heard, and I see its trademark white beak snuffling through vegetation, black body shuffling through the weeds. A brown duck pops her head above a tangle of leaves. But the most active animal life is only a few yards from where I stand. Writhing and jiving like a spine of jerky vertebrae is a line of black tadpoles, tails waggling as the creatures guzzle the soft matter hanging from a stem curled above and below the surface.

The tadpole conga is a dance of quivering twitches and manic tails, as the limbless larvae feast before shooting from plant to plant, lending the scene the look of a kind of amphibious pinball machine. I watch as one splits from the band, swimming towards a lily pad, upon which one of the tadpole's cousins lies, like a dark shadow on a purple heart.

Leading down from the pond is a wide, grassy expanse graced by occasional trees, like the horse chestnut facing me as I stroll towards the lake, hanging high over the park. Here, the lake is mostly the preserve of pleasure boaters, but at its perimeters can be seen families of geese and ducks, with coots and their young thronging at the edge. I watch two juveniles, feathers already turning fur-like grey, ducking and dodging under the current, wary parents circling them. On each side, children pedal past in large pink contraptions, like combinations of boats and dodgem cars, *their* wary parents watching from the lakeside and calling out encouragement or warnings to go safe.

From here, the park declines into a wooded area, a stream running over rocks, the lip of the lake just visible through overhanging leaves. I pass this part of the landscape often on the train, make out the shapes of boats peeping through the trees. On foot, it is possible to cut through the woodlands and find yourself within an enclosed patch of flat land. Secluded among a haven of beech and bluebells, it is easy to imagine you are miles from civilisation, rather than just a few yards from a busy road, a railway and a busy park flowing with families and day-trippers.

A stately green steam train comes winding by along a specially laid track, the Shibden Park land train, ferrying passengers of all ages across the park. Other than this passing vehicle, I am alone in this shady corner, silent but for the occasional chirpings of unseen birds. Sun, half-hidden by the trees, polishes the path of odd-sized paving stones before me in a sheen of spring sunlight.

Straight ahead, the way through the woods forks into a footpath alongside the rail tracks, well beaten and leading to the familiar outline of the lake, and an overgrown and uphill rut into the woods, which is uneven, narrow and heading into the cover of thick green trees. I stop for a breather, the ornate train slips into the distance, and the dappled light of early evening comes inching through the trees. I point my feet north, cleave a path through ravelled branches, and take the road less travelled.

Wildlife by Train

Early morning, heading east, somewhere between Sowerby Bridge and Huddersfield, I watch through the window of a train, as fields catch the light of the early spring sun, and grass glitters beneath a cobweb-coloured fog.

With the frisky innocence of newborn lambs, deer dance in and out of bushes whose greening foliage tumbles down towards the river.

By the Calder, we ride over the bridges criss-crossing the valley. At Mirfield, where the tracks are split by a kind of central reservation overflowing with valerian and buttercups, the wharf is a jumble of boats, preceded by a rough-and-ready weir, where the river rushes over stones and reels below the railway towards Ravensthorpe. This is a good place to see herons. Often, on a morning, I've noticed one poised on the corner of the weir, impervious and calm. I keep an eye peeled in the evenings, too, as the train approaches Sowerby Bridge, where one of the gangly birds may be seen straight and still as a flagpole on the river's edge, eyes fixed down to spy for fish.

The Calder Valley is fortunate to be covered by a fairly extensive railway network, and my journeys up and down its rural and urban routes have always offered opportunities to spot wildlife. In spring, the rabbits bound by as we pass fields and farmland, the swans glide over ponds outside Mirfield, Ravensthorpe's raven-black cormorants brood by the water's edge at Ladywood Lakes, and deer can be glimpsed further away as we skim the fringes of their woodland worlds.

Wildlife by Train

Watching wildlife from the windows of a train is like being granted temporary visions of a transient reality, front-row seats before an ever-shifting stage of seasonally changing backdrops. Outside Dewsbury, there is a mass of birches, which in winter look like a rack of skeletons, pocked with pigeons. As the year nudges towards spring, their high branches start to lighten with bright green.

It is invigorating to see hillsides thickening with grass, waterbirds multiplying on canals and streams, unexpected flowers springing up by the tracks. Only this evening, I marvelled at a hawthorn, white against a green array of birch, beech and sycamore.

Sometimes, commuting at the crack of dawn, or heading home at the end of a heavy day, or simply in the course of a random journey on the rails, the most familiar of scenes can offer up new sights. When the ears are not besieged by phone calls, the loutish shouts of drunks or noisy tannoy messages, when the mind is too tired to yield even to the temptations of a book, the simple, old-fashioned pastime of looking out of the window can conjure up surprising magic.

Travelling by train is one of the best ways to encounter those in-between spaces where wildlife often thrives. Overlooked and disregarded by many, the margins of our landscapes – the 'edgelands' explored by poets Paul Farley and Michael Symmons Roberts in their book of that name – these bookends of towns and outskirts of estates, these rubbled borderlands and remnants of an industrial past promote ecological diversity. Largely free from human interference, the edges are a hinterland for shyer wildlife like deer, and also host to wildflowers, fungi and innumerable insects.

One of my favourite junctures on the Calder Valley lines is the Copley Viaduct near Sowerby Bridge, which provides panoramic views of the surrounding country. It also happens that the train often stops here for minutes at a time to make way for late expresses hurtling above. For all the irritation of these delays, the traveller at least is offered a prolonged opportunity for observation.

Sometimes, on the lower tracks, we stop at a particular halfway point between the viaduct and station, a short walk from the town, yet a place that feels secluded and off-grid. A disused signalman's hut stands in venerable decay, and tracks curl into the distance in zigzags of silver-grey. Seemingly plonked in the middle of a bare expanse, a metal sign proclaims the spot as Greetland Junction. Shuttered by Beeching, a station stood nearby from 1897 until 1962. Now the locale is a wilderness, the sort of flat backwater ignored by guidebooks, but rich with native flora, busy pools and spring greenery.

Further along, where Copley interweaves with the periphery of Sowerby Bridge, the hillside bristles with gorse. I love to sit and gaze through the glass at this long display of fiery flowers. Early on, it's a patchy presence, clumps here, clusters there, vivid with colour, like tiny bonfires in the winter chill. By mid-April, it coats the hill like tinsel, a braid of breeze-ruffled bunting, brightening my journey home. In the early evening, these frills of spiky gold seem to reach for the skies, prickling the misty sunsets.

Riding through the evening by train looking from the window at catkins on the bushes, watching fields whir by in blurs of green, is a privilege beyond price. These May evenings, when I'm half-asleep from the chugging rhythm of the train, it

Wildlife by Train

is a simple pleasure for me to watch the world go by in fleeting frames of riversides and trees, wildflower meadows, and the occasional flap of wings lifting into sky.

Heptonstall

When describing the civil parish of Heptonstall in one of his finest poems, Ted Hughes paid particular attention to its gravestones and regular rainfall – and even likened it to a skull. Yet despite the preponderance of tombs, the gothic ruins of a thirteenth-century church and, yes, the rain, which lets up only for intervals even in spring, I have never seen the place in these glum terms myself.

If anything, Heptonstall evokes images of sunlight and floral colour in my mind, though that may well be due to my habit of visiting during spring and summer, when the steep roads and hillsides leading up to it are less tricky propositions for travel on foot than when coated in snow and ice.

This warm May Sunday saw me approach from the old packhorse route, known locally as 'the buttress', a cobbled climb whose steepness is notable even in a region defined by that very quality, and perhaps rivalled only by the ludicrously steep Fall Lane connecting Sowerby Bridge to Norland. Once this formidable slog has been surmounted, I thread intermittent paths and narrow stone steps through the rugous woods, emerging at the familiar huddle of cottages, cafés, pubs and post office that is the village of Heptonstall, in all its rustic cosiness.

From Smithwell Lane, the view looks out onto a splay of buttercups and dandelions, sweeping towards masses of green trees. In the distance, the coned spire of Stoodley Pike impales the gathering clouds.

Heptonstall

Of course, it would be folly to deny the air of mediaeval mystery that pervades its environs, and Heptonstall is synonymous with the remains of the Church of St Thomas à Becket. The grey-stoned bones of the ruins loom from the brow of a hill; the structure has been derelict since storm damage in 1847 and is now a shell whose flooring is a composite of long stone slabs and graves, in between which sprouts unkempt grass.

The tower is rectangular, like a hollowed-out stone pillar, slightly tilted, and home to a flock of pigeons. Birds flit from ledge to ledge, or alight on the crenellations to gaze down into a dark shaft of cobwebbed stone. In the right light, there's a lime-green quality – moss on the columns, visible also from the tower's interior, like a matted fungus slowly devouring it.

This tower, like much of the rest of the ruins, seems cast in no single colour – instead, its stone is scrawled in various shades of of coal black, rain grey and lichen green. Like a dragon, it stands ungainly but proud, a stone pillar in Pennine earth, rising at an angle to its neighbour and replacement, the stately parish church, from which the ruins are separated by a graveyard rich in grasses, dandelions and dock. The area is busy with birds. A blackbird saunters over dropped sycamore flowers, which cover a gravestone like a carpet. Elsewhere, sparrows move from tomb to tomb, blue tits frequent the holly bushes, a magpie fastens its claws to a fence. In front of the newer church, a goat willow stands plump with leaf, catching the sun.

In the adjoining cemetery, the graves are filed in wavy lines, and back out onto moorland. The American poet Sylvia Plath, whose husband Ted Hughes hailed from nearby Mytholmroyd, is buried there.

A Year in the Calder Valley

Sylvia Plath's visits to the valley initially sparked the poet's fascination with the Brontës, and prompted her to extol what she saw as the perfection of its wildness and loneliness in a letter to her mother in September 1956. Over time, perhaps seen through the prism of a deteriorating private life, as well as contrasting with her native Massachusetts, her visions of the valley devolved into a series of foreboding portraits. This is exemplified by poems like 'Hardcastle Crags', named after that that outcrop of rocks and woods a few miles down the valley, with its mill pond and its miles of ferny splendour, in which the author recalls dark hills and black stone.

In his poem 'Stubbing Wharfe', depicting an evening scene in nearby Hebden Bridge, Ted Hughes relays drily how, despite his own embrace of the area's landscape, his wife noticed only the valley's blackness. Nonetheless, she was buried in the cemetery at Heptonstall following her death by suicide in London, in 1963.

Today, the scene is one of peaceful, flourishing abundance, gravestones rising through long grass in a peaceful spot. The poet's grave lies behind a host of forget-me-nots, whose tiny blue flowers dance in today's breeze. As ever, there are flowers placed on top of the stone – the latest are buttercups, upturned to the sun. 'Even amidst fierce flames,' reads the gravestone's capitalised inscription, 'the golden lotus can be planted.'

Leaving the graveyard, I approach the quiet hamlets of Slack and Colden and follow a course cut into woodlands that plunge down the sheep-strewn valley towards Lumb Bank. The woods are a cage of birch, matted with moss. Take a snickety path through the bushes, and you'll be picking your way along a sloping trove of bluebells and wild garlic, the frilly white crystals of its flowers twinkling like woodland sprites.

Slugs are plentiful here, stuffed into the grass beneath your feet. As I scale the slanting banks, grabbing onto roots and stalks, I see the pudgy black bodies of *Arion ater*, the rubicund tubes of *Arion rufus* and other, unidentified, slugs.

Eventually, this corridor of woodland opens out into a sun-bathed platform of open rock. Below, outspread like the fan of a fantastical peacock, lies an explosion of verdure, a boundless array of trees, as far as the eye can see, hooded by an ocean of pearly clouds. Nowhere else have I seen such a huge expanse of unbroken green, such a magnificent display of trees. The scene has overwhelmed me. I stand in a kind of daze, like a pioneer contemplating a new land, basking in the natural majesty of this rich, uniquely beautiful valley.

Acknowledgements

Thanks to the *Halifax Courier* and Sowerby Bridge's *Go Local* for allowing several previously published pieces to be included in this book, and to Chris Lever of National World and Rachel Taylor for their support.